Teacher's Book

A RESOURCE FOR PLANNING AND TEACHING

Level K WOW! Wonder of Words

Senior Authors J. David Cooper, John J. Pikulski

Authors Kathryn H. Au, Margarita Calderón, Jacqueline C. Comas, Marjorie Y. Lipson, J. Sabrina Mims, Susan E. Page, Sheila W. Valencia, MaryEllen Vogt

Consultants Dolores Malcolm, Tina Saldivar, Shane Templeton

INVITATIONS TO LITERACY

Houghton Mifflin Company • Boston

Atlanta • Dallas • Geneva, Illinois • Palo Alto • Princeton

Acknowledgments

Grateful acknowledgment is made for permission to reprint copyrighted material as follows:

Golden Bear, by Ruth Young, illustrated by Rachel Isadora. Text copyright © 1992 by Ruth Young. Illustrations copyright © 1992 by Rachel Isadora. Music and lyrics copyright © 1992 by Ruth Young. Reprinted by permission of Viking Penguin, a division of Penguin Books USA, Inc.

I Love Animals, by Flora McDonnell. Copyright © 1994 by Flora McDonnell. Reprinted by permission of Candlewick Press Inc., 2067 Massachusetts Avenue, Cambridge, MA 02140.

"I Love Little Pussy," traditional.

Ira Sleeps Over, by Bernard Waber. Copyright © 1972 by Bernard Waber. Reprinted by permission of Houghton Mifflin Company. All rights reserved.

My Big Dictionary, by the Editors of the American Heritage Dictionaries, illustrated by Pamela Cote. Copyright © 1994 by Houghton Mifflin Company. All rights reserved.

"My Teddy Bear," from *Farther Than Far*, by Margaret Hillert. Copyright © 1969 by Margaret Hillert. Reprinted by permission of the author.

"Night Comes," from *A Bunch of Poems and Verses*, by Beatrice Schenk de Regniers. Copyright © 1977 by Beatrice Schenk de Regniers. Reprinted by permission of Marian Reiner for the author.

The Rain Puddle, by Adelaide Holl, illustrated by Roger Duvoisin. Text copyright © 1965 by Adelaide Holl. Illustrations copyright © 1965 by Roger Duvoisin. Reprinted by permission of Lothrop, Lee & Shepard Books, a division of William Morrow & Company, Inc. and The Bodley Head.

Spots, Feathers, and Curly Tails, by Nancy Tafuri. Copyright © 1988 by Nancy Tafuri. Reprinted by permission of Greenwillow Books, a division of William Morrow & Company, Inc.

"When All the World's Asleep," from *Rings and Things*, by Anita E. Posey. Copyright © 1967 by The Macmillan Publishing Co. Reprinted by permission of the Executor of the Estate of Anita E. Posey.

Where Does the Brown Bear Go? by Nicki Weiss. Copyright © 1989 by Monica J. Weiss. Reprinted by permission of Greenwillow Books, a division of William Morrow & Company, Inc.

Credits

Photography

THEME: In the Barnyard: Banta Digital Group, pp. T4, T5, T6, T7, T14, T34, T62, T64; Dave Desroches, pp. T55, T58; Tracey Wheeler, pp. T13, T26, T28, T29, T31, T33, T57, T59, T61, T63, T81, T83, T85, T86, T87, T91, T92; Tony Scarpetta, pp. T27, T31, T53, T61, T85, T87; Kathy Copeland, pp. T27, T30, T32, T33, T52, T53, T54, T57, T60, T62, T85, T90, T92, T96; Karen Ahola, pp. T29, T81; Tom Tafuri, p. T34; Photo Courtesy of Walker Books, Ltd., p. T64

THEME: Nighttime: Banta Digital Group, pp. T98, T99, T100, T101, T108, T125, T130, T132, T150, T151, T156, T157, T160, T162, T190; Dave Desroches, p. T155; Tracey Wheeler, pp. T107, T125, T127, T128, T129, T152, T153, T155, T157, T159, T160, T161, T181, T183, T185, T189, T190, T194; Tony Scarpetta, pp. T126, T154, T158, T182, T183, T185; Kathy Copeland, pp. T127, T131, T151, T152, T155, T157, T178, T179, T180, T185, T188, T190; Photo Courtesy of Houghton Mifflin Trade Books, p. T108

Printed in U.S.A.

ISBN: 0-395-79544-3

23456789-B-99 98 97

In the Barnyard

Table of Contents
THEME: In the Barnyard

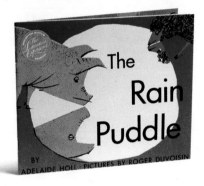

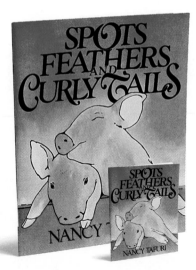

Big Books LITERATURE FOR WHOLE CLASS AND SMALL GROUP INSTRUCTION

by Flora McDonnell

fiction

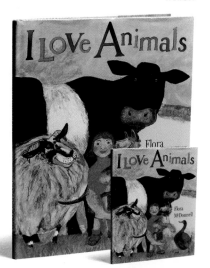

WATCH ME READ Books PRACTICE FOR HIGH-FREQUENCY WORDS AND PHONICS SKILLS

Each title is also available in black and white. This version includes a home activity.

Bibliography

Books for the Library Corner

 Multicultural

 Science/Health

 Math

 Social Studies

 Music

 Art

700 Kids on Grandpa's Farm
 by Ann Morris
Dutton 1994 (32p)
This photo essay follows the activities of those who operate a goat farm.

Barnyard Banter
by Denise Fleming
Holt 1994 (32p)
All of the farm animals are clucking and mewing and braying and chirping except for Goose, who is missing.

The Farm Counting Book
 by Jane Miller
Simon 1983 (32p) also paper
An introduction to simple counting concepts using color photos of farm animals.

Wake Up, Wake Up!
by Brian and Rebecca Wildsmith
Harcourt 1993 (16p)
In turn, all of the farm animals make noise until the farmer wakes up to feed them.

Have You Seen My Duckling?
by Nancy Tafuri
Greenwillow 1984 (24p) Puffin 1986 paper
A mother duck searches for her adventuresome duckling. **Available in Spanish as ¿Has visto a mi patito?**

A Hat for Minerva Louise
by Janet M. Stoeke
Dutton 1994 (24p)
A hen named Minerva Louise finds a hat to keep her warm as she plays in the snow.

Early Morning in the Barn
by Nancy Tafuri
Greenwillow 1983 (24p) also paper
Three cheeping chicks leave their henhouse to visit all the other animals waking up on the farm.

See How They Grow: Calf
 by Mary Ling
Dorling Kindersley 1993 (24p)
Sequential photographs show the growth of a calf over a period of months. *See others in series*

Rosie's Walk
by Pat Hutchins
Macmillan 1968 (32p) also paper
A hungry fox slinks behind an unsuspecting hen as she walks around the barnyard.

On the Farm
 Dorling Kindersley 1994 (32p)
Photographs of animals and farm equipment accompany simple facts about farm life.

On the Farm

In the Spring
by Craig Brown
Greenwillow 1994 (24p)
Spring signals the arrival of many animal babies on the farm.

Smart, Clean Pigs
by Allan Fowler
Childrens 1993 (32p)
Photographs and simple information about pigs. **Available in Spanish as Los limpios e inteligentes cerdos.**

This Is the Farmer
by Nancy Tafuri
Greenwillow 1994 (24p)
A farmer sets off a chain of events when he kisses his wife.

Books for Teacher Read Aloud

The Thing That Bothered Farmer Brown
by Teri Sloat
Orchard 1995 (32p)
A humming mosquito keeps Farmer Brown and all the barn animals from a good night's sleep.

You Silly Goose
by Ellen Stoll Walsh
Harcourt 1992 (32p)
A silly goose mistakes a mouse for a fox.

On the Farm
by Lee Bennett Hopkins
Little, Brown 1991 (32p)
An illustrated collection of poems about farm life by well-known poets like Myra Cohn Livingston and David McCord.

The Surprise Family
by Lynn Reiser
Greenwillow 1994 (32p)
A chicken becomes a proud and protective surrogate mother for some ducklings.

When the Rooster Crowed
by Patricia Lillie
Greenwillow 1991 (32p)
In this cumulative tale, a tired farmer wants just a few more minutes to sleep.

Zinnia and Dot
by Lisa Campbell Ernst
Viking 1992 (32p) Puffin 1995 paper
Two feuding hens agree to share the hatching of the one remaining egg after a weasel attack.

No Milk!
by Jennifer A. Ericsson
Morrow 1993 (32p)
A city boy tries to cajole a cow into giving him milk.

My Hen Is Dancing
by Karen Wallace
Candlewick 1994 (32p)
A boy tells all about his pet hen, including what she eats and how she keeps her feathers clean.

The Hee-Haw River
by Dee Lillegard
Holt 1995 (32p)
A farmer wife's comment about a river sets in motion a chaotic chain of events.

The New Baby Calf
by Edith Newlin Chase
Scholastic 1991 (32p)
Plasticine illustrations accompany a poem about a baby calf.
Available in Spanish as
El ternero recién nacido.

Quacky Duck
by Paul and Emma Rogers
Orion 1995 (32p)
A constantly quacking duck annoys the other animals until she disappears and things become too quiet.

Books for Shared Reading

Rise and Shine!
by Nancy White Carlstrom
Harper 1993 (32p)
Rhyming verse describes what animals say, eat, and do during the course of a day.

The Very Busy Spider
by Eric Carle
Putnam 1989 (32p)
A horse and a cow and other farm animals try to divert an industrious spider from spinning her web.

Big Red Barn
by Margaret Wise Brown
Harper 1989 (32p)
Rhyming text tells the story of the animals that live in a big red barn.

Fiddle-i-Fee: A Farmyard Song for the Very Young

by Melissa Sweet
Little, Brown 1992 (32p)
also paper
A merry parade of animals joins a boy in a ramble around a farmyard.

Oh, What a Noisy Farm!
by Harriet Ziefert
Tambourine 1994 (32p)
A bull chasing a cow sets off a noisy chase around the farm.

The Wonderful Feast
by Esphyr Slobodkina
Greenwillow 1993 (32p)
After Farmer Jones feeds his horse, other farmyard animals feast on the leftovers.

The Farmer in the Dell

by Kathy Parkinson
Whitman 1988 (32p)
This illustrated version of the nursery rhyme is accompanied by music.

Cat Goes Fiddle-i-Fee
by Paul Galdone
Clarion 1985 (32p) also paper
A boy feeds the hen, the sheep, the horse, and other farm animals in this nursery rhyme.

Jane Yolen's Old MacDonald Songbook
by Jane Yolen
Boyds Mills (96p) 1994
A collection of forty-three favorite songs from the barnyard.

Technology Resources

Computer Software

Internet See the Houghton Mifflin Internet resources for additional bibliographic entries and theme-related activities.

Video Cassettes

Have You Seen My Duckling? *by Nancy Tafuri.* Am. Sch. Pub.

Rosie's Walk *by Pat Hutchins.* Weston Woods

Animals on the Farm *Nat'l Geo*

Audio Cassettes

Just Me *by Marie Hall Ets.* Live Oak Media

The Midnight Farm *by Reeve Lindbergh.* Weston Woods

Filmstrips

Petunia, Beware! *by Roger Duvoisin.* Am. Sch. Pub.

A Treeful of Pigs *by Arnold Lobel.* Am. Sch. Pub.

Animals Around You: Farm Animals *Nat'l Geo*

AV addresses are in Teacher's Handbook, H14–H15.

Theme at a Glance

Reading/Listening Center

Selections	Comprehension Skills and Strategies	Phonemic Awareness	Phonics/Decoding	Concepts About Print	
The Rain Puddle	✓ Drawing conclusions, T25 Role-playing to draw conclusions, T28 Versions of the story, T28 Drawing fun conclusions, T28 Reading strategies, T18, T20, T24 **Rereading and responding,** T26–T27	✓ Identifying alliteratives, T19, T29 Picture card match-up, T29 Identifying different areas of a farm, T29		Animals found in the barnyard, T21	
Spots, Feathers, and Curly Tails	✓ Making predictions, T39 Making predictions about animals, T54 Predicting a book's content by looking at the cover, T54 Reading *Who Is the Beast?* and making predictions, T54 Reading strategies, T38, T42, T44, T46, T50 **Rereading and responding,** T52–T53		✓ Initial *h*, T45 Decoding *h* words, T55 Pantomiming, T55 Solving a puzzle, T55 Using My Big Dictionary, T56 Naming pictures, T56 Creating a farm collage, T56	✓ First letter in written words, T41 Role-playing teacher, T57 Making a farm collage, T57 Framing individual words, T57	
I Love Animals	✓ Classify/categorize, T79 Creating a feather/fur chart, T82 Categorizing picture cards, T82 Classifying food, T82 Reading strategies, T68, T70, T74, T78 **Rereading and responding,** T80–T81		✓ Initial *d*, T69 Initial *h*, T71 ✓ Phonogram -*at*, T77 Decoding *d* words, T83 Identifying words that begin with *d*, T83 Spelling *d* words, T83 Phonogram -*at* riddles, T84 Forming words with -*at*, T84 Words that rhyme with *cat*, T84	Last letter in written words, T73 Word find, T85 Word collage, T85 Identifying last letters, T85	

✓ *Indicates Tested Skills. See page T11 for assessment options.*

Theme Concept	Pacing	Multi-Age Classroom
Each animal has its own features, characteristics, and behaviors.	This theme is designed to take 2½ to 3 weeks, depending on your students' needs and interests.	This theme can be used in conjunction with a theme found in another grade level. Grade 1: Something Fishy

Writing/Language Center   Cross-Curricular Center

Vocabulary	Listening	Oral Language	Writing	Content Areas
		Identifying animals and their sounds, T30 Discussing the animals' responses to the owl, T30 Chart of barnyard animals, T30	Barnyard chart, T31 Barnyard books, T31 Describing farm animals, T31	**Math:** learning about different shapes, T32 **Science:** experiment with a rain puddle, T32 **Social Studies:** learning about farm chores, T33 **Creative Movement/Music:** playing an action-mirroring game to music, T33
✔ High-frequency word: *the*, T51 High-frequency words: *the, said*, T58 Finding *the*, T58 Forming new sentences, T58	What's found on a farm, T59 Listening for information, T59 Recognizing different animal names, T59	Describing an animal, T60 Making animal comparisons, T60 Names of body parts, T60	Class story, T37 Riddle book, T61 Caring for a farm animal, T61 Describing farm animals, T61	**Science/Math:** measuring ingredients to make dairy products, T62 **Art:** designing a feathered bird, T62 **Science:** creating a farm animal chart, T63 **Music/Movement:** playing follow the leader, T63
✔ High-frequency word: *I*, T75 Writing *I love* sentences, T86 Word search, T86 Reading a take-home story, T86	Finding what doesn't belong, T87 Listening for beginning sounds, T87 Listening to read along tape, T87	Favorite animals, T90 Language play, T90 Using exact action words, T90	Class book, T67 Scrapbooks, T89 Collecting words, T89 Group recipe, T91 Describing animals, T91 Special invitations, T91	**Math:** learning about patterns, T92 **Social Studies:** food products that come from a farm, T92 **Music/Movement:** moving creatively to sounds of animals, T93 **Science:** observing hay, T93

Meeting Individual Needs

Key to Meeting Individual Needs

 ### Students Acquiring English

Activities and notes throughout the lesson plans offer strategies to help children understand the selections and lessons.

 ### Challenge

Challenge activities and notes throughout the lesson plans suggest additional activities to stimulate critical and creative thinking.

 ### Extra Support

Activities and notes throughout the lesson plans offer additional strategies to help children experience success.

Managing Instruction

Independent Work: Self-Selected Reading

Self-selected reading is one of the best choices for independent work. Begin by building the following routine:

Place many easy and engaging books in baskets on the tables or workspaces in your classroom. Select a book from one of the baskets and begin with five minutes of reading aloud to your students, followed by five minutes of free reading. Close the time with two or three minutes of sharing by individual students. Gradually increase the amount of time for self-selected reading to ten, then fifteen minutes. At the fifteen minute level, begin your work with small flexible groups.

For further information on this and other Managing Instruction topics, see the *Professional Development Handbook.*

Performance Standards

During this theme, children will

- *explore the barnyard setting*
- *monitor how well they understand their reading*
- *evaluate and retell or summarize each selection*
- *apply comprehension skills: Drawing Conclusions, Making Predictions, Categorize/Classify*
- *identify alliteratives and words beginning with the sounds for* h *and* d

- *recognize the high-frequency words* the *and* I
- *recognize words with the phonogram* -at
- *identify word boundaries*
- *write a story*

Students Acquiring English	Challenge	Extra Support
Develop Key Concepts Children focus on Key Concepts through role-playing, making charts and collages, and picture previews.	**Apply Critical Thinking** Children apply critical thinking by drawing conclusions, making predictions, and categorizing and classifying.	**Receive Increased Instructional Time** Practice activities in the Reading/Learning Center provide support with drawing conclusions, making predictions, and categorizing and classifying. Children also receive additional work on identifying alliteratives.
Expand Vocabulary Throughout the theme, children use context and picture clues, discuss meanings, and model definitions. Children expand their vocabulary to include animal sounds.	**Explore Topics of Interest** Activities that motivate further exploration include making a chart of barnyard babies, doing an experiment with evaporation, naming farm chores, and learning about farm products.	**Provide Independent Reading** Children choose to explore books and to read independently when exciting, theme-related literature is made available (see Bibliography, T6-T7).
Act as a Resource Children are asked to share the sounds animals make in their native languages.	**Engage in Creative Thinking** Opportunities for creative expression include making a farm collage, creating an owl mask, and creating a patterned series.	

Additional Resources

Invitaciones

Develop bi-literacy with this integrated reading/language arts program in Spanish. Provides authentic literature and real-world resources from Spanish-speaking cultures.

Language Support

Translations of Big Books in Chinese, Hmong, Khmer, and Vietnamese. *Teacher's Booklet* provides instructional support in English.

Students Acquiring English Handbook

Guidelines, strategies, and additional instruction for students acquiring English.

Planning for Assessment

Informal Assessment

Observation Checklists

- Concepts About Print/Book Handling
- Responding to Literature and Decoding Behaviors and Strategies
- Writing Behaviors and Stages of Temporary Spelling
- Listening and Speaking Behaviors
- Story Retelling and Rereading

Literacy Activity Book

Recommended pages for students' portfolios:
- Beginning Sounds, p. 65
- Personal Response, p. 66
- Comprehension: Making Predictions, p. 69
- Language Patterns, p. 74
- Phonics/Decoding: *d*, p. 77

Retellings–Oral/Written

- *Teacher's Assessment Handbook*

Formal Assessment

Kindergarten Literacy Survey

Evaluates children's literacy development. Provides holistic indicator of children's ability with
- Shared Reading/Constructing Meaning
- Concepts About Print
- Phonemic Awareness
- Emergent Writing

Kindergarten Literacy Survey

Theme Skills Test

- Categorize/Classify
- Letter Sounds *h* and *d*
- High-Frequency Words: *the* and *I*
- Phonogram *-at*

Theme Skills Test

Portfolio Assessment

The portfolio icon signals portfolio opportunities throughout the theme.

Additional Portfolio Tips:
- Evaluating Progress in Emergent Writing, T95

Launching the Theme

See the Houghton Mifflin **Internet** resources for additional activities.

Song Tape for In the Barnyard: "Old MacDonald Had a Farm"

INTERACTIVE TEACHING

Warm-up

Singing the Theme Song

- Play "Old MacDonald Had a Farm" (for lyrics see the Teacher's Handbook, page H10) and invite children to sing along.

- Introduce the concept of a *barnyard*, noting that many farms have a barn where some of the animals live. Say that the open area outside and around the barn is called the barnyard. It is where children would most likely see lots of farm animals.

- Encourage children to name other animals Old MacDonald might have on his farm. Children can sing the song again, substituting other animals' names and the sounds they make.

Interactive Bulletin Board

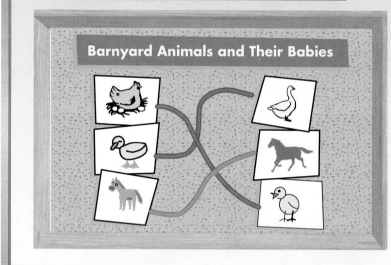

Barnyard Animals and Their Babies

Barnyard Animals and Their Babies
Children create a bulletin board of barnyard animals and their babies.

- Have children find (or draw) pictures of the animals featured in the selections, both adult animals and their young.
- Have them put adult animals on the left side of the board and their young on the right.
- Children can use yarn to connect each adult animal to its baby.

See the *Home/Community Connections Booklet* for theme-related materials.

Portfolio Opportunity

The Portfolio Opportunity icon highlights portfolio opportunities throughout the theme.

Ongoing Project

Our Own Little Farm

Invite children to create their own miniature farms on the sand table or other large surface. Suggestions for creating farm structures and farm animals are provided throughout the theme. Children might

- Bring in toy animals from home to represent some of the farm animals.
- Look at the "Farm Places" Poster for ideas about how to arrange things.

Children can take visitors on a tour of their miniature farm.

Choices for Centers

Creating Centers

Use these activities to create learning centers in the classroom.

Reading/Listening Center

- At the Pond, T28
- Judging a Book by Its Cover, T54
- What / Love, T86

Language/Writing Center

- Barnyard Chart, T31
- Let's Do "The Hokey Pokey," T60
- Mine's the Best, T90

Cross-Curricular Center

- Science: The Rain Puddle Experiment, T32
- Art: Design a Feathered Friend, T62
- Social Studies: Where Does Our Food Come From? T92

READ ALOUD

SELECTION:

The Rain Puddle

by Adelaide Holl
illustrated by Roger Duvoisin

Other Books by Adelaide Holl

My Weekly Reader Picture Word Book

Other Books Illustrated by Roger Duvoisin

The Camel Who Took a Walk
Petunia

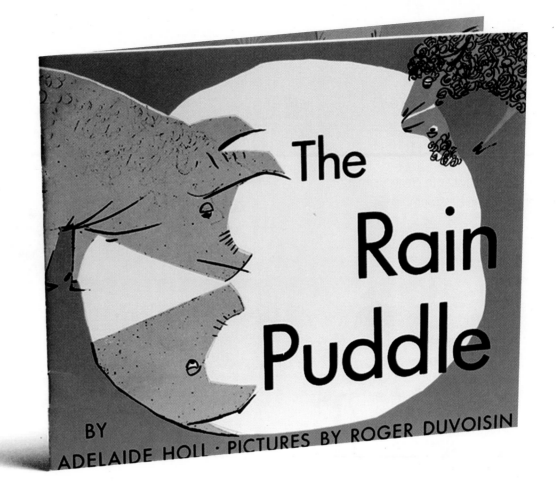

• **Best Books for Children**

Selection Summary

When hen sees her reflection in the rain puddle, she thinks another hen has fallen in. Away she runs, seeking help from turkey. When turkey looks in, he, too, sees his own reflection. And so it goes, with each animal —until there's a whole barnyard full of animals reflected in the puddle. But then the sun comes out and dries up the puddle. All but the wise old owl think the animals have finally climbed out to safety.

Lesson Planning Guide

	Skill/Strategy Instruction	Meeting Individual Needs	Lesson Resources
1 **Introduce** *the* **Literature** *Pacing: 1 day*	**Preparing to Listen and Write** Warm-up/Build Background, T16 Read Aloud, T16	Choices for Rereading, T17	**Poster** The Eensy Weensy Spider, T16 *Literacy Activity Book* Personal Response, p. 63
2 **Interact** *with* **Literature** *Pacing: 1-2 days*	**Reading Strategies** Monitor, T18, T24 Self-Question, T18, T24 Evaluate, T20 Summarize, T18 **Minilessons** ✔ Identifying Alliteratives, T19 Animals Found in the Barnyard, T21 ✔ Drawing Conclusions, T25	Students Acquiring English, T18, T23, T27 Extra Support, T19, T20, T21, T25, T26 Challenge, T22, T24, T26 Rereading and Responding, T26–T27	Story Props, T27 See the Houghton Mifflin **Internet** resources for additional activities
3 **Instruct** *and* **Integrate** *Pacing: 1-2 days*	**Reading/Listening Center,** Comprehension, T28 Phonemic Awareness, T29 **Language/Writing Center,** Oral Language, T30 Writing, T31 **Cross-Curricular Center,** Cross-Curricular Activities, T32–T33	Challenge, T30, T32 Extra Support, T28, T29 Students Acquiring English, T31	**Poster** Farm Places, T29 Letter, Word, and Picture Cards, T29, T30 *Literacy Activity Book* Comprehension, p. 64 Phonemic Awareness, p. 65 See the Houghton Mifflin **Internet** resources for additional activities

✔ *Indicates Tested Skills. See page T11 for assessment options.*

1

Introduce
the
Literature

Preparing to Listen and Write

Poster

Eensy Weensy Spider

The eensy, weensy spider
Went up the waterspout.

Down came the rain
And washed the spider out

Out came the sun
And dried up all the rain,

And the eensy, weensy spider
Went up the spout again.

Literacy Activity Book, p. 63

Dear Family,
Look through old magazines to find pictures of farm animals your child can name. Together you might want to cut out the pictures and paste them on pages to make your own book about farm animals.

The Rain Puddle
PERSONAL RESPONSE
Children draw pictures of favorite animals from The Rain Puddle. They may wish to write or dictate words to label their pictures.

INTERACTIVE LEARNING

Warm-up/Build Background

Sharing a Song
- Display the poster "The Eensy Weensy Spider." (See music in Teacher's Handbook, page H11.)
- Invite children to listen and follow the words as you sing the song.
- Encourage children to chime in with you as you sing the song again.
- You may want to teach children the fingerplay for "The Eensy Weensy Spider."
- Ask if children have ever noticed how rain on the street or in puddles dries up once it stops raining and the sun comes out. Explain that children will learn more about why this happens later on. (See page T32.)

Read Aloud
LAB, p. 63

Preview and Predict
- Display the cover of *The Rain Puddle*. Read aloud the title and the author's and illustrator's names.
- Ask children to name the animals they see on the cover. (pig, sheep) Note that the large round white shape is a rain puddle. Ask what each animal sees when it looks into the rain puddle. (its own reflection) If children seem confused about this, ask them to look at their own reflections in a small hand mirror. Then explain that sometimes you can see yourself reflected in a puddle.
- Read aloud pages 2-5 of the story. Ask children what they think hen *really* sees in the rain puddle. Contrast this with what hen *thinks* she sees.
- Ask children to predict what hen will do.

Read

Read the story, pausing every few pages for children to predict what each animal will see and to match their predictions with what actually happens. As you read, encourage children to raise their hands if they hear something they don't understand.

Personal Response

Home Connection Have children complete *Literacy Activity Book* page 63 to show which farm animal was their favorite. Encourage children to tell about the animals they drew. Invite children to work with family members to create their own book on farm animals.

Choices for Rereading

Picture Pauses

As you reread, pause after each spread and invite children to talk about the illustration. Have them sharpen their notice of details by asking them to describe everything they see in the pictures. Ask children why they think the artist made the cow yellow, the turkey purple, and the sheep blue. After reading page 16, see if children notice that the color of the animals reflected in the puddle is lighter. Why? After page 18, have children tell how the artist shows the animals are excited and how he shows movement.

More Choices for Rereading

Rereadings provide varied, repeated experiences with the literature so that children can make its language and content their own. The following rereading choices appear on page T26.

- What's the Solution?
- How Would *You* Feel?
- Wise Old Owl Speaks Up

Looking and Telling

To help children recall the sequence of events, have them sit in a circle and take turns retelling the story as you show the illustrations in *The Rain Puddle*. Give children a small hand mirror to pass (and look into at appropriate times) as a way to designate the storyteller.

Acting It Out

To involve children with the characters, have them pantomime the characters' actions as you read the story aloud. You might use a large piece of aluminum foil to simulate the rain puddle. Be sure to remove the "puddle" after reading page 18.

Interact *with* Literature

READ ALOUD

Reading Strategies

▶ **Monitor/ Self-Question Summarize**

Teacher Modeling Tell children that when they listen to a story or read on their own, they should think about the things that happen. They should ask themselves: Do the things that happen make sense? Could the things that happen take place in real life?

Think Aloud

Sometimes when I am reading, I'm not sure that I really understand everything that takes place in the story. When this happens, one thing I do is to think about whether what happens in the story could take place in real life. Sometimes, things in a story could really happen, but other things in the very same story are only make believe. If I'm still confused, I go back and read again and look at the pictures.

Purpose Setting

Encourage children to remember the important parts of the story as you reread it so they can tell a friend what it is about. Tell children to draw or write something to help them remember each animal as you reread the story. Allow time for this as you reread.

Plump hen was picking and pecking in the meadow grass.

"Cluck, cluck! Cluck, cluck!" she said softly to herself.

2

3

All at once, she came to a rain puddle.

"Dear me!" she cried. "A plump little hen has fallen into the water!"

And away she ran calling, "Awk, awk! Cut-a-cut! Cut-a-cut! Cut-a-cut!"

4

5

QuickREFERENCE

⭐⭐⭐ **Multicultural Link**

Children who speak languages other than English might name farm animals and their sounds in those languages. In Spanish, for example, the hen, *la gallina (gah* EE*na)* would say *cio cio (CEE*oh).*

Students Acquiring English
MEETING INDIVIDUAL NEEDS

The Rain Puddle is a good story for students acquiring English because the pictures provide strong clues.

Vocabulary

Explain that a *meadow* is a grassy field. Farm animals may eat the grass in a meadow. Hens *peck,* or pick things up with their beaks. What might hens peck for in a meadow? (food: seeds, small bugs)

Turkey was eating corn in the barnyard.

"Come at once!" called plump hen. "A hen is in the rain puddle!"

Away went turkey to see for himself.

6

7

"Gobble-obble-obble!" he cried when he looked in. "It is not a plump hen. It is a big, bright turkey gobbler!"

8

9

Science Link

Ask children to note ways in which the hen and the turkey are alike. (Both have beaks, wings, similar feet and heads.) Ask what covers the bodies of these animals. (feathers) Help children conclude that both are birds.

Extra Support

MEETING INDIVIDUAL NEEDS

You may want to paraphrase the last sentence on page 6, which uses inverted word order, for children. Explain that the sentence means that the turkey went away (to the rain puddle) to see if there really was a hen in it.

Phonemic Awareness

TESTED SKILL

Identifying Alliteratives

Teach/Model

Read aloud the first sentence on page 2, emphasizing the words *picking* and *pecking*. Then model recognizing alliterative words.

Think Aloud

When I read the words *picking* and *pecking,* I notice something special. Both words begin with the same sound. They begin with the sound for *p.*

Have children repeat *picking* and *pecking,* listening for their beginning sound.

Reread the next sentence on page 2. Have children repeat the word that names the sound the hen made. (cluck) Then note that *said* and *softly* have the same beginning sound, the sound for *s.* Ask children to repeat *said* and *softly,* listening for their beginning sound.

Practice/Apply

Ask children to listen carefully as you say three words. They should repeat the two words that begin with the same sound. Say:

| fat | pig | fallen |

Repeat with these sets of words:

| cow | cut | tree |
| full | fan | water |

SKILL FINDER *Identifying Alliteratives,* page T29

2 The Rain Puddle

THEME: IN THE BARNYARD

Interact
with
Literature

READ ALOUD

Reading Strategies

▶ **Evaluate**

Teacher Modeling Model how to think about the animals and their behavior.

Think Aloud

I know that even though the animals in this story look like real animals you might see on a farm there are things about them that are make-believe. They talk. They also act silly. They think other animals have fallen into the puddle and they get excited.

Ask children if they agree that the animals are silly. Have them decide if their behavior is very silly or just a little silly.

Pig was crunching red apples in the orchard. He heard the news. Off he waddled to take a look.

"Snort, snort! Oink, oink! They are both wrong," pig said to himself. "It is a beautiful, fat pig that has fallen into the rain puddle. I must get help at once!"

QuickREFERENCE

 MEETING INDIVIDUAL NEEDS **Extra Support**

Vocabulary Discuss the meanings of these words: *orchard* (place where fruits grow), *snort* and *oink* (sound words), *waddled* (a way of walking), *nibbling* (taking little bites), and *clover* (a plant). Demonstrate waddling and nibbling.

T20 *The Rain Puddle*

Read Aloud pp. 10–13

Curly sheep was nibbling sweet clover in the pasture, and cow was softly chewing her cud under a shady tree.

"What is going on?" they said to one another. "Let us go and see."

14

15

They found all the other animals crowded around the puddle together. "A whole barnyard full of animals has fallen into the water," they all exclaimed. "We must run for help!"

16

Vocabulary Explain that a *pasture* is a field where animals are put so they can eat the grass growing there. If children ask about *cud,* explain that a cow brings up food from its stomach for a second chewing. This food is called *cud.*

MINILESSON

Concept Development
Animals Found in the Barnyard

Teach/Model

Ask children to point to and identify each animal in the picture on page 17. Elicit that all these animals live on the farm in the story.

Have children "perform" the different sounds the animals make and tell the different things they eat.

Then assign the following roles to volunteers:

hen	sheep
turkey	cow
pig	

Reread pages 2-14, asking each volunteer to recall his/her sound and food. Then have children role-play their animals. For example:

PIG: This apple tastes so good. Snort, snort! Oink, oink!

Practice/Apply

Have children suggest sounds and foods for the horse and the donkey in the picture on page 17. Repeat the role-play to include these animals.

SKILL FINDER *Animals on the Farm, page T29*

Interact *with* Literature

While all the animals were running about in great excitement, the sun came out. The sun shone warm and bright. It dried the rain puddle all up.

18

19

Plump hen stopped running around in circles and cried, "Awk, awk! Cut, cut! Look! The animals have all climbed out safely!"

And away she went to pick and peck in the meadow grass.

20

21

QuickREFERENCE

Challenge

Ask children if they think the animals would react the same way if they looked in a rain puddle again. (yes) Why? (The animals still haven't realized that they were looking at their own reflections.)

Journal

Have children draw what they would see if they looked in a rain puddle.

"Gobble-obble-obble! So they have!" agreed turkey. And off he went to eat corn in the barnyard.

22

23

"You are quite right," snorted pig. And he waddled off to crunch red apples in the orchard.

24

QuickREFERENCE

Science Link

Invite children to share times when they have used the sun or something warm to dry something. Have they ever put wet laundry on a clothes line? Or put wet shoes near a radiator? Or sat in the sun in a wet bathing suit?

Students Acquiring English

Explain what turkey meant when he said, "So they have." He meant that they—all the animals—have climbed out safely.

Interact *with* Literature

 READ ALOUD

Reading Strategies

 ### Monitor/Self-Question

Teacher Modeling Help children understand why owl chuckled.

Think Aloud

Why did owl chuckle? The picture shows he is up high on a tree branch. That is why he can see that the animals are just looking at themselves in the puddle. He chuckles because he thinks they are silly.

 ### Summarize

Recall all the animals in the story. Then model how to summarize.

Think Aloud

If I wanted to tell a friend about this story, I would tell about the most important things that happen in it. Instead of naming each animal, I would just say that lots of different farm animals looked into a rain puddle, one by one, and thought they saw an animal that had fallen in. Only one wise animal wasn't fooled!

Curly sheep said, "Baaaa, baaaa," and went back to nibble sweet clover in the pasture.

26

27

"Moooo, moooo!" said cow. "All of the animals escaped!" And off she went to find a shady tree and to chew her cud.

28

29

QuickREFERENCE

 Challenge

After reading page 30, ask children why they think the owl is described as wise. (He knows the animals were looking at their own reflections.)

Self-Assessment

Have children ask themselves:

• If I get confused while reading and the pictures don't help me, do I talk things over with someone else?

Wise old owl looked down from a tree above and chuckled to himself.

30

Comprehension

Drawing Conclusions

TESTED SKILL

Teach/Model

Model how to draw conclusions based on story information and what someone would know from personal experiences.

Think Aloud

All the animals that looked into the rain puddle said they saw other animals that were the same as themselves. The hen said she saw a hen because she saw an animal with a beak, wings, and feathers. The pig said he saw a pig because he could see a fat pink body and a curly tail. They just did not figure out that they were just seeing themselves in the water.

Practice/Apply

Have children pretend that another animal looked into the puddle. He saw a very little gray body, a pink nose, and a long skinny tail. This animal said "squeak, squeak" when he saw himself in the puddle. Ask: *What animal looked into the puddle?* (mouse)

SKILL FINDER

Role-Playing to Draw Conclusions, page T28

Minilessons, Themes 2, 7, and 12

Visual Literacy

Be sure children realize that owl was watching all the time—from a tree *above* the puddle. Point out that the artist shows the puddle (and the other animals) very close up—so the tree, which is farther away, isn't in the other pictures.

MEETING INDIVIDUAL NEEDS **Extra Support**

Word Meaning Demonstrate what chuckling is. Be sure children understand that chuckling is a kind of laughing. Invite children to try chuckling, too.

Science Link

Explain to children that owls are nocturnal animals. (They hunt at night and sleep during the day.) Help children name some other nocturnal animals. (bats, raccoons, rats)

Interact
with
Literature

Rereading

Choices for Rereading

What's the Solution?

Extra Support To help children develop an understanding of story problems and solutions, pause as you read to ask these questions:

- page 17: What do the story animals think they see in the rain puddle? (a whole barnyard full of animals)

  What do they do to try to solve this problem? (They run for help.)

- page 18: Do the animals actually get help? (no) Who or what did solve the problem? How? (the sun—by drying the puddle up)

- page 30: Who was the only one who knew how the problem was really solved? (the owl)

How Would *You* Feel?

To help children identify story characters' feelings, pause after reading pages 4, 8, 12, and 16 to ask children how they think the animals felt. Read with as much expression as you can muster to help convey the animals' amazement and alarm.

Wise Old Owl Speaks Up

Challenge To introduce the notion of point of view, have children retell the story page by page from the owl's point of view. You might make an owl mask, which can be passed along to designate the storyteller. As you display each illustration, children should tell what the owl sees and thinks.

Informal Assessment

- Use Story Talk or the retelling activity to assess children's understanding of the story.
- As children retell the story page by page, note their book handling skills.

Responding

Choices for Responding

Story Talk

Have children work in small groups of two or three to discuss these questions:

- What do you think of the animals in this story? Which ones are silly? Which one is not silly? How do you know?

- Why do you think the wise old owl didn't tell what he knew about reflections?

Students Acquiring English Allow children with very limited English proficiency to work in same language groupings to discuss the questions in their primary languages.

Personal Response: Rain Puddle Fun

Invite children to draw pictures of what they would do if they found a rain puddle. They might draw what they would see if they looked into the puddle. Encourage children to write or dictate sentences that tell about their pictures.

Acting Out with Stand-up Characters

Children will enjoy using the stand-up animal props and the mirror to retell the story. Assemble the stand-up figures by sliding the bottom edges into the bases. Have children take turns standing each animal on the edge of the mirror and telling what the animal sees, says, and does in the story. Encourage children to make sounds to show how the animals in the story are feeling.

Materials
Story Retelling Props: stand-up characters, mirror (See Teacher's Handbook, page H2.)

Portfolio Opportunity

For a sample of children's ability to respond to a story, save children's responses to Rain Puddle Fun.

Instruct *and* **Integrate**

Comprehension

Owl said, _____

The Rain Puddle
COMPREHENSION Inferences: Drawing Conclusions

Practice Activities

Role-Playing to Draw Conclusions

LAB, p.64

Extra Support Take the part of wise old owl in the story; children will be the other farm animals. Display page 17 of *The Rain Puddle*, and ask each animal, in turn, what he or she sees in the rain puddle. (Children should respond that each animal sees an animal that looks just like him- or herself.)

Then ask questions such as these:

- Tell me, sheep, what kind of animal do you see?
- What about you, cow? Do you see an animal that looks just like you?
- Tell me, turkey. What do you see? Do you think it's strange that you see another turkey—and not a horse or a pig?

As an extension, children may enjoy taking the part of the owl and asking the farm animals why they no longer see themselves after the puddle dries up.

Have children complete *Literacy Activity Book* page 64.

At the Pond

To check children's ability to draw conclusions, ask groups of children to imagine that on her way back to the hen house one day, hen passes by a pond. She looks into the water and sees—a plump little hen in the water. Have groups discuss what they think would happen. Ask each group to act out the scene for the class, using the story line from *The Rain Puddle*.

Fun Conclusions

Write the following on the board, and read the sentences for children.

All birds have feathers.
Hen is a bird.
Hen has _____.

Lead children to conclude that since hen is a kind of bird, she must have feathers.

Invite children to help you construct similar sentences about other birds in the story. They might change the word *hen* to *turkey* or *owl.*

Informal Assessment

As children complete the activities on these pages, note

- whether they are able to draw conclusions about the story.
- their ability to recognize words that begin with the same sound.

Phonemic Awareness

Practice Activities

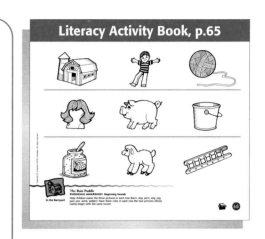

Identifying Alliteratives

LAB, p.65

Extra Support Invite children to help you name some of the animals in the story. Point out that you will suggest two names for each animal. They should choose the one that begins like the first word you say.

- Hen: Holly *or* Molly?
- Turkey: Jed *or* Ted?
- Pig: Paul *or* Saul?
- Cow: Marla *or* Carla?
- Horse: Hattie *or* Mattie?
- Donkey: Dick *or* Rick?

Have children complete *Literacy Activity Book* page 65.

Poster

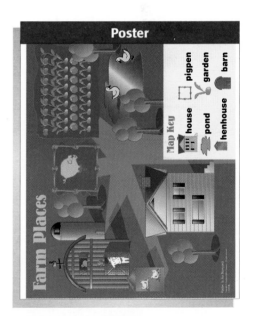

Picture Card Match-Up

Display Picture Cards *cat, cow*, and *bat*. Have children name the pictures. Ask which names begin with the same sound. (*cat* and *cow*)

Repeat with these sets of Picture Cards:

- red, bed, bus (*bed* and *bus*)
- lock, socks, seal (*socks* and *seal*)
- bear, pear, pig (*pear* and *pig*)
- jet, net, jam (*jet* and *jam*)
- hook, book, horn (*hook* and *horn*)
- fan, pan, fox (*fan* and *fox*)

Animals on the Farm

Concept Development Use the map on the poster "Farm Places" to identify different areas of the farm. Point to each symbol in the key, and discuss its meaning. Show children how to use the key to find on the map such things as the barn, the barnyard area, the farmer's house, and the pond.

Have children use toy farm animals, or cut-out drawings of animals with stand-up tabs attached to the backs, to show where on a farm the animals might be found. Children might moo, oink, squawk, and so on as they place the animals on the map.

Portfolio Opportunity

Save *Literacy Activity Book* page 65 as a record of children's ability to note alliteratives. You might tape-record children's version of At the Pond to assess children's ability to draw conclusions.

Instruct
and
Integrate

Oral Language

Choices for Oral Language

Animal Talk

Review the animal sounds mentioned in the story. Then have children brainstorm with you a list of other animals they might find on a farm. Have them start by looking at the animals pictured on pages 17 and 19, and remind them not to forget the owl. Then they might add others, such as a duck, a goat, the farmer's dog or cat. Work with children to identify each new animal's sound and add each sound word to the list. Display Word Card *said* and have children read it. Suggest children use the word and entries from your list to form oral sentences that tell the sounds different animals make.

Materials
- Word Card *said*

Believe It Or Not!

MEETING INDIVIDUAL NEEDS

Challenge Ask children to think about what the animals might say if owl tried to explain to them what they really had seen in the rain puddle—just their own reflections. Would they believe owl? What could owl do to prove to them that his explanation was correct? Encourage groups of children to express their ideas. Then invite each group to dictate a sentence to tell what owl would say to his barnyard friends and what they would say back.

Barnyard Babies

Ask children what hen's babies are called. (chicks) Then help children make a chart of barnyard babies.

ANIMAL	BABY
hen	chick
pig	piglet
sheep	lamb
cow	calf
horse	foal (colt, filly)

Have children find pictures for the bulletin board display: *Barnyard Animals and Their Babies.*

Informal Assessment

- As children complete the oral language activities, note the ease with which they participate in group discussions.

- Use the writing activities to note children's familiarity with animals and their characteristics.

 # Writing

Choices for Writing

Barnyard Chart

Invite children to help you make a chart of the farm animals in the story. Begin by listing the animals, as shown in the first column below. Then reread the story, and have children raise their hands when they hear what each animal is eating and what sounds it makes. Add these to the chart. As you write the words, read them aloud for children.

Animal	What It Eats	What It Says
hen	seeds in grass	Cluck, cluck!
turkey	corn	Gobble-obble
pig	apples	Snort, snort
sheep	clover	Baaaa, baaa!
cow	cud	Moooo, moooo!

Barnyard Books

Make several barnyard-animal-shape books with sturdy covers and blank pages. Invite children to use the pages in each book to write something about that animal. Children can look through informational books about barnyard animals for some ideas. They might write or dictate for the cow-shaped book, for example, *Cows moo* or *Cows eat grass*. Encourage children to share their writing. You may like to place the books in the Reading/Listening Center for children to enjoy independently.

Describing Farm Animals

Ask children to choose one animal from *The Rain Puddle* to describe in writing. You might make this a class activity, with each child dictating a sentence to describe the animal and its characteristics. Display children's descriptions on a bulletin board, together with a picture of the animal.

Students Acquiring English Have children who speak another language demonstrate animal sounds in their language. Ask other children to guess what animal makes that sound.

Portfolio Opportunity

You may wish to save children's barnyard books as a sample of their written work.

3

Cross-Curricular Activities

Math

Tiptoeing Through the Barnyard

Draw on or paste to each cutout shape a picture of one of the animals from the story. Mix the shapes and place them on the floor. Have children name each animal and tell on what kind of shape it is shown. Use a pattern, such as: *The hen is on a triangle*. Then have children take off their shoes and take turns walking through the "barnyard" and among the animals.

As you call out a shape name, have the child find one example of it and step on it. Have him or her name the animal and then proceed to the next shape you call out. In addition to giving practice in discriminating shapes, this activity provides an opportunity to observe children's balance and coordination.

Materials
- cardboard or oak tag shape cutouts (several circles, squares, triangles)
- farm animal pictures

Science

The Rain Puddle Experiment

Have children experiment to find out how long it takes for a puddle to evaporate.

- Place a shallow pan or pie plate in a sunny location.
- Add about 1/4 inch of water to the pan.
- Observe what happens.

Children might record what they notice each day on a chart. They can also mark with an X each day on a classroom calendar until the water evaporates.

Challenge Place a pan of water in the shade. Have children record what happens and then compare the results with the earlier experiment.

Social Studies

All In a Day's Work

Talk with children about the chores most farmers perform during the day, guiding children to understand that the farmer must get up very early to feed and water the animals, milk cows, collect hens' eggs, and then go to work in the fields, either planting crops or picking them. If possible, show pictures of farmers at work. Then invite children to role-play some of the activities discussed. Ask: *Which part of the farmer's day do you think would be the hardest? the most tiring? the most pleasant?*

Creative Movement

Musical Mirrors

Assign each child a partner, and have partners face each other. Appoint one partner to be the "leader." The leader can be any animal from *The Rain Puddle*. Appoint the other to be the "mirror."

As you play the music, all leaders should move about like the animals from the story. The mirrors should try to copy the leaders' actions as closely as possible. (You may want to limit the space within which a leader can move; a circle of yarn can be used to define boundaries.)

Have children switch roles, and repeat the activity.

Materials
- recording of instrumental music

BIG BOOK

SELECTION:

Spots Feathers and Curly Tails

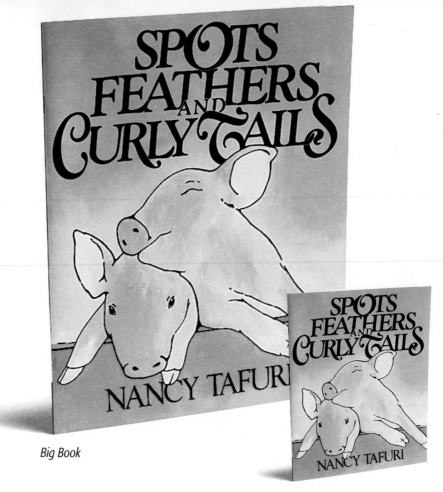

Big Book

Little Big Book

by Nancy Tafuri

Other Books by Nancy Tafuri

Early Morning in the Barn
Have You Seen My Duckling?
In a Red House

- **Child Study Children's Book Award**
- **Best Books for Children**

Selection Summary

What has spots? What has feathers? In this engaging "puzzle" book, children identify different barnyard animals from various features of their bodies. Each answer is provided on a two-page spread.

Lesson Planning Guide

	Skill/Strategy Instruction	Meeting Individual Needs	Lesson Resources
1 **Introduce** *the* **Literature** *Pacing: 1 day*	**Shared Reading and Writing** Warm-up/Build Background, T36 Shared Reading, T36 Shared Writing, T37	**Choices for Rereading,** T37 **Students Acquiring English,** T37	**Poster** Five Little Ducks, T36 *Literacy Activity Book* Personal Response, p. 66
2 **Interact** *with* **Literature** *Pacing: 1–2 days*	**Reading Strategies** Predict/Infer, T38, T42 Monitor, T38 Think About Words, T44 Evaluate, T46, T50 Summarize, T50 **Minilessons** ✔ Making Predictions, T39 ✔ First Letter in Written Words, T41 ✔ Initial *h*, T45 ✔ High-Frequency Word: *the*, T51	**Extra Support,** T48, T50, T51, T52 **Challenge,** T40, T41, T46 **Students Acquiring English,** T53 **Rereading and Responding,** T52–T53	**Letter, Word, and Picture Cards,** T45, T51 *Literacy Activity Book* Language Patterns, p. 67 **Audio Tape** for In the Barnyard: *Spots Feathers and Curly Tails* See the Houghton Mifflin **Internet** resources for additional activities
3 **Instruct** *and* **Integrate** *Pacing: 1–2 days*	**Reading/Listening Center,** Comprehension, T54 Phonics/Decoding, T55–T56 Concepts About Print, T57 Vocabulary, T58 Listening, T59 **Language/Writing Center,** Oral Language, T60 Writing, T61 **Cross-Curricular Center,** Cross-Curricular Activities, T62–T63	**Extra Support,** T54, T55, T57, T58 **Challenge,** T56 **Students Acquiring English,** T60	**Poster** Five Little Ducks, T58 **Letter, Word, and Picture Cards,** T54, T55, T56, T58, T59 **My Big Dictionary,** T56 *Literacy Activity Book* Comprehension, p. 69 Phonics/Decoding, p. 71 Vocabulary, p. 72 See the Houghton Mifflin **Internet** resources for additional activities

✔ *Indicates Tested Skills. See page T11 for assessment options.*

Introduce *the* Literature

Shared Reading and Writing

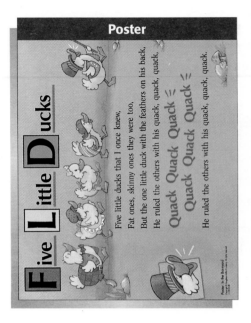

Poster

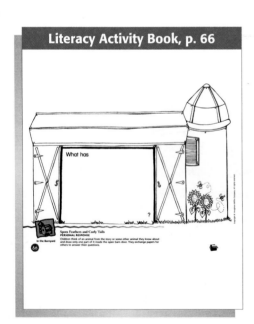

Literacy Activity Book, p. 66

INTERACTIVE LEARNING

Warm-up/Build Background

Share a Song
- Display the poster "Five Little Ducks."

- Invite children to listen to and follow along with the words to "Five Little Ducks," a song about some barnyard animals.

- Play the song for children. Then play it again and encourage children to sing along, especially on the quack, quack, quacks.

- Children may also enjoy performing the fingerplay as they sing.

Shared Reading

LAB, p. 66

Preview and Predict
- Display *Spots Feathers and Curly Tails*. Read aloud the title. Explain that Nancy Tafuri wrote the words and drew the pictures.

- Ask children to identify the animals on the cover. Ask where they think this story might take place. (on a farm, in the barnyard)

- Remind children of the farm animals they read about in *The Rain Puddle*. Ask if they think they will meet any of these same animals in *Spots Feathers and Curly Tails*.

- Read pages 4-5 of the selection. Ask if children can guess what farm animal has spots. Point out that only *part* of the animal is shown on page 5. Then read pages 6-7 to see if children's predictions are right.

Read Together
- Read the selection aloud, encouraging children to use word and picture clues to guess what each new animal is.

- As you read, invite children to talk about the pictures. Answer any questions they may have about the animals or what they are doing.

Personal Response

Have children complete *Literacy Activity Book* page 66 to show a favorite farm animal from the story and to challenge classmates to solve their own version of a farm-animal "puzzle."

Shared Writing: *A Class Story*

Brainstorming   Invite children to select a favorite barnyard animal to write about. Help them brainstorm ideas about that animal's life on the farm. Make a word web to help organize the ideas.

Favorite Animal

duck
pig
cow*

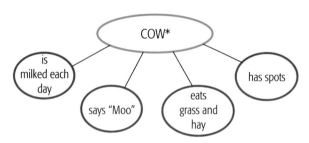

Drafting   Have children contribute sentences to the class story. Record their suggestions on chart paper. Model how to keep to the topic, if necessary.

Think Aloud

That's a good sentence, but it doesn't tell about cows. All the sentences in our story should tell about cows. *Cows* is our topic for right now.

Publishing   **Students Acquiring English** Drafting together as a class enables students acquiring English to contribute more or less depending on their proficiency level.

Have volunteers make illustrations to go with the class story. Then display children's work on a bulletin board titled "Barnyard Friends."

Choices for Rereading

You may want to use one or more of the choices for rereading that appear on page **T52**.

- Recognizing Language Patterns
- Echo Reading
- Listen and Read!
- What Has Spots? MOOO!

Portfolio Opportunity

Save examples of the writing children do independently on self-selected topics. Save *Literacy Activity Book* page 66 as a record of children's response to the literature.

Interact
with
Literature

BIG BOOK

Reading Strategies

▶ **Predict/Infer**
Monitor

Discussion Review with children the things good readers do to help them understand and enjoy a story. Recall that the first time they read *Spots Feathers and Curly Tails*, they tried to figure out what animal would appear next. This is called making predictions, and good readers do it all the time.

Discuss with children that good readers *think* while they are reading. They ask if what they are reading makes sense. Ask if children think that the sentence about the cows on pages 6-7 makes sense. Ask if they have ever seen a cow with spots. Point out that you have seen such cows, so you agree with what the author says here.

Purpose Setting

Ask children to think about whether or not *they* agree with the author as they reread the rest of the selection with you.

What
has
spots?

4

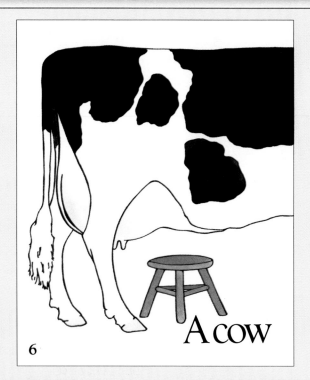

A cow

6

QuickREFERENCE

Visual Literacy

Ask what part of the animal is shown in the picture on page 5. (the back part) Discuss why the author chose to include only part of the animal. Lead children to conclude that Nancy Tafuri wanted her book to be like a guessing game.

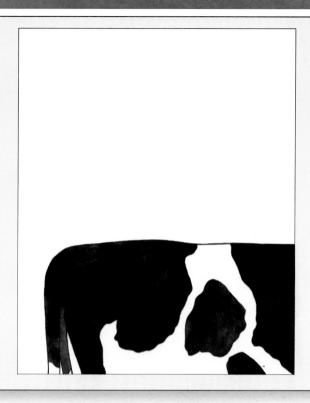

has spots.

7

MINILESSON

Comprehension

Making Predictions

 TESTED SKILL

Teach/Model

Read aloud the question on page 4. Then use the following Think Aloud to model how to predict what the answer will be.

Think Aloud

The question asks "What has spots?" I know that leopards have spots, and some butterflies have spots. But I can tell by this animal's tail and the shape of its back that it's not a leopard or a butterfly. And this book is about farm animals. I know that cows are farm animals. I know that some cows have spots. I think that the animal is a cow.

Turn the page, and show the picture of the cow. Ask if children think your prediction was correct.

Practice/Apply

Read page 8, and ask children what clues help the reader to answer this question.

 SKILL FINDER

Making Predictions, page T54

Minilessons, Theme 2

Social Studies Link

Ask children to find the milking stool and the pail in the picture. Explain that one way to milk a cow is to sit next to it and pull on its udders so milk comes out into a pail. (Another is to hook up the udders to a machine.)

✏️ Journal

Suggest that children either draw or write to record which animals they read about.

⭐⭐⭐ Multicultural Link

Help children identify foods that are made from milk. Ask if their families eat many products made from milk. Explain that certain cultural groups believe that dairy products are hard to digest.

BIG BOOK

What
has
feathers?

8

A chicken

10

has feathers.

Concepts About Print

TESTED SKILL

First Letter in Written Words

Teach/Model

Reread the sentence on pages 10-11 for children. Frame the word *chicken* with your hands. Explain that this group of letters is the word *chicken*.

Think Aloud

If I look carefully at the letters in *chicken,* I see that the first letter is *c.* (Point to the initial *c.*) The word *chicken* begins with the letter *c.*

Follow a similar procedure for *has* and *feathers.* Frame each word for children, and read it aloud. Then have volunteers point to and name the first letter in each word.

Practice/Apply

Have children find the first letter in each word in the question on page 4. Then have them find the first letter in the words *cow* and *spots* on pages 6-7.

SKILL FINDER   *Playing Teacher,* page T57

MEETING INDIVIDUAL NEEDS
Challenge

Help children give the specific names to the animals pictured on pages 10-11:
• mother chicken–hen
• father chicken–rooster
• baby chickens–chicks

Math Link

Ask children to count to find the number of animals pictured on pages 10-11. (six) Ask how many of the animals are baby chicks. (four)

Science Link

Review that in *The Rain Puddle*, the hen pecked for seeds in the meadow grass. Ask what one baby chick is doing in the picture on page 10. (pulling a worm) Point out how the chick pulls the worm from the ground.

Interact
with
Literature

Reading Strategies

▶ **Predict/Infer**

Discussion Talk with children about what the piglets are doing on pages 14 and 15. (eating) Ask children what this lets them know about how the piglets are feeling. (They are hungry.) Talk about how the piglets will probably feel after they are finished eating.

What
has a
curly tail?

12

A pig

14

QuickREFERENCE

Visual Literacy

Discuss what part of the animal is shown in the picture on page 13. (back part) Discuss what is meant by a *curly* tail, if necessary.

Concept Review

Animal Sounds Ask if children recall the sounds animals made in *The Rain Puddle*. Have volunteers make the sounds of a cow, a chicken, and a pig.

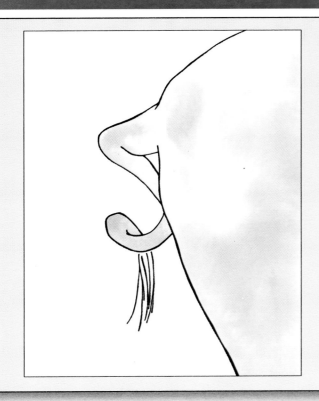

has a curly tail. 15

Math Link

Ask children to count the number of piglets in the picture on pages 14-15. (There are four; one piglet's head is hidden.)

Science Link

Recall with children that cows give milk. Explain that mammals such as cows and pigs feed their babies with their milk. Point out that the piglets in the picture are getting milk from their mother.

Interact
with
Literature

BIG BOOK

What
has
a mane?

16

A horse

18

Reading Strategies

▶ **Think About Words**

Display pages 18 and 19 and discuss how children can figure out *mane*.

The story says: *A horse has a ___.*

● **What makes sense** This word names something that a horse has.

● **Sounds for letters** Point to the word *mane*, noting it begins with *m*. Which word begins with the sound for *m* and names something that a horse has? *(mane)*

● **Picture clues** The horse in the picture has long hair on the back of its head and neck, a mane. I think the word is *mane*.

Reread the sentences on pages 18-19. Ask children if the word *mane* makes sense.

Quick**REFERENCE**

Visual Literacy

Ask children what part of the horse is shown in the picture on page 17. (front part or head) Contrast this with the part of the pig shown on page 13.

Phonics/Decoding Review

Read the word *mane*, noting the sound for initial *m*. The sound a cow makes—*mooo*—also begins with /m/. Ask children to say "mooo" when they hear /m/ words. Say: *mane, foal, tail, milk, must.*

has a mane. 19

Phonics/Decoding

Initial *h*

Teach/Model

Read aloud the sentence on page 16, pointing to the words as you say them. Frame *has* and ask children to name the first letter. *(h)* Have children say *has*, listening for the beginning sound. Conclude that *h* stands for the sound at the beginning of *has*.

Display Magic Picture *horse*.

Materials
● Picture Card: *horse*

Explain to children that Magic Picture *horse* can help them remember the sound for *h*. Have children say *has* and *horse*, listening for the beginning sounds. Then ask them to find the word *horse* on page 18.

Practice/Apply

Read pages 26-27. Ask children to name the two words that begin like *horse*. *(has, horns)* Ask volunteers to point to the letter h at the beginning of each word.

SKILL FINDER
Decoding H *Words,* pages T55, T71

Minilessons, Theme 6

Social Studies Link

Invite children who have ridden a horse or a pony to tell about the experience. Then explain that before there were cars, people often used horses to get from place to place. Ask if they know of anyone who still uses horses.

Interact *with* Literature

What
has
a bill?

20

A duck

22

Reading Strategies

▶ **Evaluate**

Discussion Help children make a chart that shows the names of the animals they have read about and their features. (This will also be helpful when children summarize later.)

Animals	Features
cow	spots
chicken	feathers
pig	curly tail
horse	mane
duck	bill

Point out that children will need to add one more animal as they continue to reread the selection with you.

Then ask if children have seen real animals with the "parts" listed in the chart. Confirm that each animal really does have the part mentioned in *Spots Feathers and Curly Tails*.

QuickREFERENCE

Visual Literacy

Ask what part of the animal is shown in the picture on page 21. (bill) Ask how a duck's bill is different from a chicken's beak.

MEETING INDIVIDUAL NEEDS **Challenge**

Multiple-Meaning Words In this selection, a *bill* is the flattened beak of a bird. Ask children what else *bill* can be. (*Bill* can also name something to be paid, as a grocery bill; paper money; or the brim of a baseball cap.)

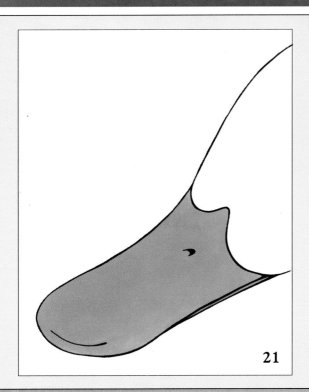

21

has a bill.

23

Science Link

Help children compare the ducks shown on pages 22-23 with the chickens on pages 10-11. How are they alike? How are they different? You might point out that a duck's webbed feet help it swim.

Interact
with
Literature

What
has
horns?

24

 A bull

26

QuickREFERENCE

Vocabulary/Visual Literacy

Explain that bulls and cows are both cattle; the bull is a male, and the cow is a female. Invite children to contrast the bull on pages 26-27 with the cow on pages 6-7.

Extra Support

Multiple-Meaning Words Help children understand that the word *horn* can mean a bony growth on an animal's head, as well as one kind of musical instrument or the thing on a car that goes *BEEP*.

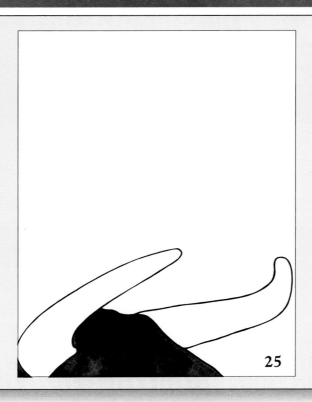

25

has horns. 27

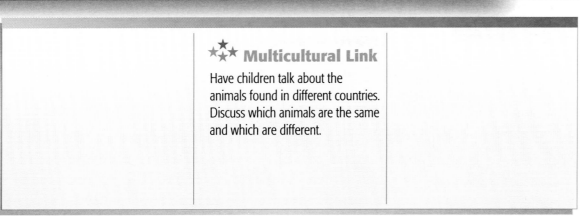

★★★ Multicultural Link

Have children talk about the animals found in different countries. Discuss which animals are the same and which are different.

Interact *with* Literature

Reading Strategies

 Summarize

Help children complete the chart of animals and their special features. Then guide them in using the chart to retell *Spots Feathers and Curly Tails.*

 Evaluate

Use these questions to help children share their feelings about the selection:

- Did you like *Spots Feathers and Curly Tails?* Why or why not?
- What new things did you learn about farm animals?
- Do you think all the things you learned are true? Why or why not?

And where do they all live?

28

On a farm

30

Self-Assessment

Have children ask themselves:
- Can I easily tell someone about the most important parts of this story?

QuickREFERENCE

Social Studies Link

Help children identify the buildings in the picture on page 29 as the top parts of the barn and the silo. Discuss that some farm animals are kept in a barn, and that food for the animals is stored in a round building called a *silo.*

 Extra Support

Pronoun Referents If children seem confused, point out that the word *they* in the question on page 28 refers to all the animals mentioned so far in *Spots Feathers and Curly Tails.*

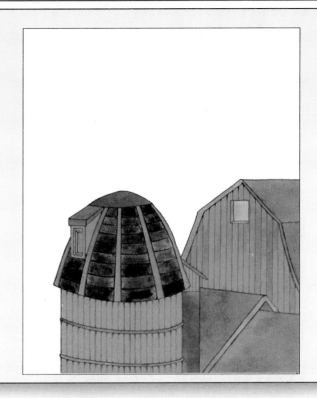

in the country. 31

Vocabulary

High-Frequency Word: *the*

TESTED SKILL

Teach/Model

Reread pages 28-31. Then display Word Card *the*.

Point to the word card and read the word for children. Ask volunteers to find *the* on pages 30-31. Have children frame it.

Use Word Card *the* and Picture Cards cow, horse, pig, and duck to construct phrases. Have children take turns reading the phrases.

Materials
- Word Card: *the*
- Picture Cards: *cow, horse, pig, duck*

Practice/Apply

Display Word Card *the*. Read the following sentences aloud, and pause for children to supply the word *the*. Then have children immediately repeat each complete sentence with you.

Mr. Green milked _____ cow.

Horses eat grass in _____ field.

SKILL FINDER

High-Frequency Words page T58

Visual Literacy

Challenge children to find all the animals they've read about in *Spots Feathers and Curly Tails* in the picture on pages 30-31.

MEETING INDIVIDUAL NEEDS **Extra Support**

Word Meaning Some children may be confused by the use of the word *country* in this context. Explain that the country is an area where few people live, so there is lots of room there for farm animals like the ones in this selection.

Interact with Literature

Rereading

Choices for Rereading

Literacy Activity Book, p.67

Recognizing Language Patterns

LAB, p. 67

Review with children the language pattern in *Spots Feathers and Curly Tails.*

> What has _____?
>
> A _____ has _____.

Invite children to brainstorm different physical features and animals that could fill in the blanks. Have children complete *Literacy Activity Book* page 67 by writing or dictating words to complete the story pattern, and then drawing pictures to accompany their writing.

Listen and Read!

 Audio Tape for In the Barnyard: *Spots Feathers and Curly Tails*

 Extra Support To promote independent reading, place copies of the Little Big Book, along with the Audio Tape, in a quiet area. Invite children to chime in with the tape as they read the selection individually or in small groups.

What Has Spots? MOO–O!

To help children interact with the selection, pause after you read each question. Invite children to make the sound of the animal that will appear in the answer.

Echo Reading

To promote fluency, reread the selection, reading each sentence aloud and then having children as a group read the sentence.

Informal Assessment

Use any of the responding activities to assess children's understanding of the selection. As children listen and read the story, note their ability to turn the pages in sequence.

Responding

Choices for Responding

Story Talk

Have children talk in small groups about the following questions:

- What did you read in *Spots Feathers and Curly Tails* that was new to you?

- Can you think of different answers to the questions in the selection? Explain your new answers.

- Which book did you like better: *The Rain Puddle* or *Spots Feathers and Curly Tails?* Explain.

- Have each group share their answers with the class.

Students Acquiring English Placing children acquiring English in mixed language groupings for this activity will help them gain proficiency.

Home Connection

Talk with children about story animals and others that have spots, feathers, or curly tails. Then have children choose one of the three features. Ask each child to draw an animal that has his or her selected feature. Encourage children to try to write captions for their pictures. Have them share their work with classmates.

Suggest that children take home their pictures and use them to tell their families about the story.

Personal Response: Create a Silly Creature

Invite children to use the different animal parts identified in the story to create and draw their own silly creatures. The creatures can look any way children want, but they must include animal parts from the story. Encourage children to give their creatures names, write or dictate sentences about them, and then share them with their classmates.

3

Instruct *and* Integrate

Comprehension

Literacy Activity Book, p.69

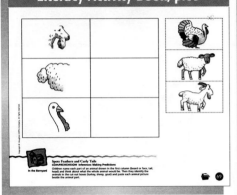

Materials

• Picture Cards: *bird, cat, fish*

Practice Activities

Making Predictions

LAB, p. 69

MEETING INDIVIDUAL NEEDS

Extra Support Ask children to tell how they were able to predict what animal would appear next in *Spots Feathers and Curly Tails*. Then display pages 8-9 of the book. After reading the question on page 8, ask:

• What kinds of farm animals have feathers? (ducks, chickens)

• What would you predict this animal to be: a duck or a chicken? (a chicken)

• Why? (The feathers are red and brown, like a chicken's.)

Cover the animals on the Picture Cards with sticky notes so that only these features are showing: bird—beak, cat—tail, fish—tail fin.

Show each one to children. Ask them to identify the body part that is showing and to guess the animal. Record children's predictions on chart paper. Then reveal the animals. Discuss how children figured out each animal. For more practice, have children complete *Literacy Activity Book* page 69.

Judging a Book by Its Cover

Show children the covers of several picture books, one at a time. Read the titles, and talk about the cover illustrations with children. Invite them to predict what they think each book is about.

Ask children which books they think they would enjoy most. Then read aloud those books, and discuss whether or not children's predictions matched what actually happened.

Who Is the Beast?

Use *Who Is the Beast?* by Keith Baker (Harcourt Brace © 1990) to give children another opportunity to make predictions. The story features jungle animals that children can identify.

Informal Assessment

• Use the Comprehension activities to assess children's ability to make predictions.

• As children complete the Phonics/ Decoding activities, note their ability to identify words that begin with the sound for *h*.

Phonics/Decoding

Practice Activities

Literacy Activity Book, p.71

Decoding *h* Words

MEETING INDIVIDUAL NEEDS

Extra Support Display Picture Cards *horse, bird,* and *hat* and help children name the pictures. Then explain that you are going to say a sentence that has one word left out of it. Children can supply the missing word by saying a picture name that makes sense in the sentence and begins with the sound for h. Read:
A ____ has a mane.

Discuss why *horse* is the correct choice and why *bird* and *hat* are not. Then repeat the procedure with Picture Cards *hippopotamus, lion, hose* and the sentence: *A ____ lives in the jungle.*

Materials

- Picture Cards:
  horse, bird, hat;
  hippopotamus,
  lion, hose

Act It Out

Whisper the word *hop* to a child. Ask the child to pantomime the action for others to guess. During the pantomime, hold up the letter card for *h*, and tell children that the word begins with the sound /h/.

Repeat the activity with these words: *hug, hang, hit, hiccup, hold, help, hide*.

It's a Puzzle!

LAB, p. 71

To provide more practice with *h* words, have children complete *Literacy Activity Book* page 71. All the puzzle pieces will fall into place to help make a special discovery.

Home Connection Invite children to bring *Literacy Activity Book* page 71 home to share with their families.

Portfolio Opportunity

For a record of children's work, save *Literacy Activity Book* page 69 to assess children's ability to make predictions.

3

Instruct *and* Integrate

Phonics/Decoding

My Big Dictionary

Practice Activities

What a Farm!

Invite children to work together to create a farm collage of pictures whose names begin with the sound for *h*. You might encourage children to look for such things as horses, hogs, hay, hens, hills, and houses.

Challenge Have children add pictures for /m/ and /s/ words to the farm collage. They might label all the pictures to show beginning sounds.

Materials

- old magazines, newspapers, and catalogs
- a large sheet of butcher paper
- scissors
- paste

My Big Dictionary

Display page 17 of *My Big Dictionary.* Read the words on page 17 aloud to children, pointing to the initial *h* and emphasizing the sound /h/ as you read. Then invite partners to work together to list other things that begin with the sound for *h*. You may want to encourage children to use temporary spellings and list their words for their journals.

Spell to Learn

Display Picture Cards for *hat* and *cat* along the chalkboard ledge. Above each, write *_at*. Have children name the pictures. Ask a volunteer to write *h* to complete the word that begins with /h/.

Repeat with Picture Cards *hook* and *book* and the letters *_ook*.

Materials

- Picture Cards: *hat, cat, hook, book*

Informal Assessment

- Note children's ability to locate pictures that begin with the sound for *h*.
- As children complete the Concepts About Print activities, assess their ability to identify the first letter of a written word.

Concepts About Print

Practice Activities

Playing Teacher

Extra Support Reread with children the words to the song "Five Little Ducks." Then invite children to take turns playing teacher as they show the class how to indicate the first letter in each word of the song. Then "the teacher" can invite others to indicate the first letter in each word while you help out as needed.

Word Collage

Provide children with old magazines and newspapers. Invite each child to cut out individual words, circle the first letter in each word, and then paste the words on construction paper to make a word collage.

Extra Support Children may prefer looking for and cutting out only those words which begin with the consonants they have learned so far.

My Own Words

Ask volunteers to dictate sentences that tell about the animals in the story. Print each sentence on chart paper. When there are several sentences, invite children to take turns framing individual words in the sentences, as they appear in sequence, and pointing out the first letter in each word.

Materials
- old magazines and newspapers
- scissors
- colored markers
- paste
- construction paper

Instruct
and
Integrate

Vocabulary

Practice Activities

Materials
● Word Cards: *said, the*

High-Frequency Words

LAB, p. 72

Give each child both Word Cards. Ask them to listen as you read several sentences. Explain that one word will be missing, and that they should hold up the missing word. Read these sentences, saying "blank" for each missing word.

● "Welcome to my farm," ____ Old MacDonald. *(said)*

● "Would you like to see ____ animals?" *(the)*

● Then he ____, "My cow gives milk." *(said)*

● With that, ____ cow began to moo. *(the)*

● "MOOO!" ____ the cow. *(said)*

Have children complete *Literacy Activity Book* page 72.

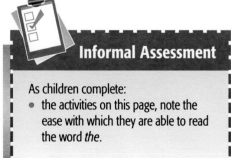

Informal Assessment

As children complete:
● the activities on this page, note the ease with which they are able to read the word *the*.

"Five Little Ducks"

Display the poster. Reread the song as children follow along. Then ask volunteers to find the word *the* in the song. It occurs five times. When they do, they should hold the Word Card over the word in the song text. Have children help you reread each sentence in which *the* is located by a volunteer.

You may like to extend the activity by writing the Mother Goose rhyme "Little Boy Blue" on chart paper and after reading it aloud having children look for the occurrences of *the*.

What Belongs to Whom?

Display the following in a pocket chart:

"My ," said the .

Have a volunteer read the sentence. Then substitute, in turn, these pairs of pictures to form new sentences: *nest, bird; carrot, rabbit; lettuce, goat; milk, cow*. Ask children to read each new sentence.

Materials
● Picture Cards: *bird, nest, carrot, rabbit, lettuce, goat, milk, cow*
● Word Cards: *my, said, the*

Listening

Practice Activities

Found on a Farm

Display the picture cards on the chalkboard ledge. Tell children to listen very carefully as you ask some questions. Ask:

- What is found on a farm?

- What has four legs and is found on a farm?

- What makes a good pet, has four legs, and is found on a farm?

- What barks, makes a good pet, has four legs, and is found on a farm?

As you ask each question, children must remove the cards that do not belong. They can then use the remaining cards to answer your questions. For example:

- **Q:** What has four legs and is found on a farm?

- **A:** A cat, a cow, a dog, a goat, a horse, a mouse, and a pig have four legs and are found on a farm.

Materials

- Picture Cards: *cat, cow, bird, bear, deer, dog, duck, fish, fox, goat, horse, kanga-roo, lion, monkey, mouse, pig, rabbit, seal, tiger, turkey, worm, yak*

Cows With Feathers? No Way!

To give children practice listening for information, reread the story, replacing the animal names with new ones. For example, in response to "What has feathers?" you might say, "A cow has feathers." Children should stop the reading as soon as they hear an error. Encourage them to replace the word you've said with the correct animal name.

Listen to the Animals

Ask children to listen as you read a short nursery rhyme. Have them raise their hands each time they hear the name of a different animal.

Bow-Wow

Bow-wow, says the dog,
Mew, mew, says the cat,
Grunt, grunt goes the hog,
And squeak goes the rat.
Tu-whu, says the owl,
Caw, caw, says the crow,
Quack, quack says the duck,
And what cuckoos say you know.

—*Mother Goose*

Portfolio Opportunity

- Save *Literacy Activity Book* page 72 as a record of children's understanding of high-frequency words.

- As children complete the Listening activities, write down some observations about each child's ability to listen for information. Place these observations in their portfolios.

3 Instruct *and* Integrate

Oral Language

Choices for Oral Language

Describe an Animal

Invite children to take turns standing in front of the class and describing a farm animal without mentioning what the animal is. Encourage children to tell:

- what the animal *looks* like
- what it might *feel* like, if touched
- what it *sounds* like

Listeners can try to guess the animal based on its description.

Let's Do "The Hokey Pokey"

Help children review the names of their body parts by playing and singing the "The Hokey Pokey." Then name an animal from the selection, and have children pretend to be that animal as you tailor the words of the "The Hokey Pokey" to the animal. For example, ducks might put in their bills, their left and right wings, and their tail feathers.

Students Acquiring English Change the animal every so often so children can learn the names of different animals' parts.

Animal Comparisons

Model for children how to form simple comparisons using *like* or *as*: *I'm fast like a horse; I'm as kind as a cow; I'm smart like an owl.* Then invite them to take turns comparing themselves to some of the animals they have read about in this story and the preceding one.

Materials
- recording of "The Hokey Pokey" (optional)

Informal Assessment

- Use Let's Do "The Hokey Pokey" to informally assess children's understanding of human and animal body parts.
- As children work on their writing assignments, note whether they are developing strong letter-sound correspondence.

Writing

Choices for Writing

My "What Has?" Riddle Book

Invite children to make their own *What Has?* riddle books. To give children ideas for the pages, share a few simple riddles with them. For example:

- What has leaves?   A tree has leaves.
- What has wheels?   A skateboard has wheels.

Provide each child with several sheets of paper. To make their books, children can write, or dictate, their questions on one side of a page and the answers on the back. Encourage children to illustrate their questions and answers.

When all riddles are complete, compile them into individual books. Children may want to make covers for their books. Invite children to work in groups and share their riddles.

Farm Choices and Chores

Tell children that youngsters who live on farms often have to share in the chores, especially helping to take care of the animals. Invite children to tell which farm animal (one from this story or any other animal) they would like to care for and why. Ask children to name one specific thing they would have to do to take care of that animal—comb its mane, milk it, and so on. Record children's ideas.

Our Best Farm Friends		
Nilda	chickens	feed them
Tony	horse	brush
Mike	goat	give water to

Word Paintings

Brainstorm with children a list of words that can describe the farm animals and record them on chart paper. Hang the word chart in the classroom. Then provide children with finger paint and finger paint paper. Invite them to draw a farm animal, and then copy a word or two from the chart that describes the animal they drew.

Portfolio Opportunity

You may wish to save children's riddle books or word paintings as a sample of their written work.

3

Instruct
and
Integrate

Cross-Curricular Activities

Science/Math

Dairy Delights

Children may enjoy seeing how milk is changed into other dairy products in these simple recipes. As you follow the recipes, encourage children to watch as you measure ingredients, noting aloud how much of each ingredient you use.

Cheese

Ingredients: two cups of milk, juice from 1/2 lemon

1. Heat the milk to nearly boiling. Remove from heat.
2. Add the lemon juice. The milk will quickly separate into curds (solid cheese) and whey (the leftover liquid).
3. Pour off the whey and eat.

Butter

Ingredients: one cup of heavy cream, salted to taste

1. Put the cream into a two-cup mayonnaise jar, screw on the lid tightly, and have children take turns shaking it until it turns to butter.
2. Spread on a cracker and eat.

Art

Design a Feathered Friend

Recall with children that chickens have feathers. Talk about other animals that have feathers. Then pass around a feather and have children describe what it is like, including how the feather looks, what it feels like, and where it might have come from.

Invite children to create their own birds by pasting feathers onto cut-out bird shapes. Tell them not to use too much paste or the feathers will get matted down.

Materials

- feathers (can be purchased from arts and crafts catalogs and stores)
- cut-out shapes of birds, including chickens and ducks
- paste

Music/Movement

Follow the Leader

Children may enjoy playing a game as they sing "Five Little Ducks."

- Children form a line behind a leader, walking like ducks as they sing the song.

- As children sing "He ruled the others...," the leader initiates a rhythmic action, such as clapping hands or stomping feet. Others in line imitate the action.

- After the last "quack," the leader goes to the end of the line, and the next child in line becomes the new leader.

Science

Featuring Farm Animals

Have children help you create a chart for the farm animals in the story.

	2 legs	4 legs	fur/hair	feathers	wings	mane	tail
horse		X	X			X	X
cow		X	X				X
chicken	X			X	X		X
pig		X	X				X
duck	X			X	X		X

Children can add a picture next to each animal's name. Help children note details about each animal, such as number of legs, body covering, and so on. Explain that if an animal has that feature, they should put an X in the box.

BIG BOOK
SELECTION:
I Love Animals

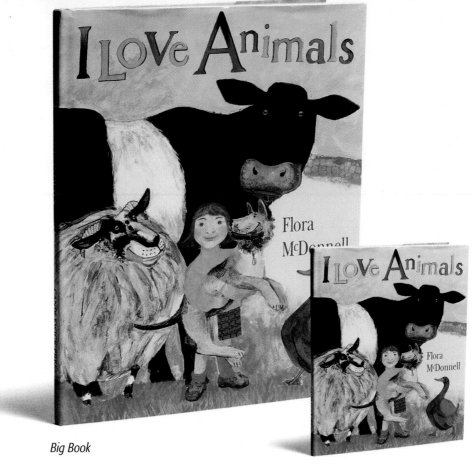

Big Book

Little Big Book

by Flora McDonnell

**Other Books by
Flora McDonnell**

I Love Boats

● **Parenting Magazine's
Reading Magic Award**

Selection Summary

The barnyard in this charming picture book bustles with activity, and a young girl expresses a joyous love for its animals. Do these exuberant animals love her too? She hopes so!

Lesson Planning Guide

	Skill/Strategy Instruction	Meeting Individual Needs	Lesson Resources
1 **Introduce** *the* **Literature** *Pacing: 1 day*	**Shared Reading and Writing** Warm-up/Build Background, T66 Shared Reading, T66 Shared Writing, T67	Choices for Rereading, T67	**Poster** I Love Little Pussy, T66 *Literacy Activity Book* Personal Response, p. 73
2 **Interact** *with* **Literature** *Pacing: 1-2 days*	**Reading Strategies** Evaluate, T68, T74, T78 Think About Words, T70 Predict/Infer, T74 **Minilessons** ✔ Initial *d*, T69 Initial *h*, T71 Last Letter in Written Words, T73 ✔ High-Frequency Word: *I*, T75 ✔ Phonogram *-at*, T77 ✔ Classify/Categorize, T79	**Extra Support,** T69, T71, T75, T80 **Challenge,** T70, T76 **Students Acquiring English,** T68, T73, T80 **Rereading and Responding,** T80–T81	**Letter, Word, and Picture Cards,** T69, T71, T75, T77 *Literacy Activity Book* Language Patterns, p. 74 📼 **Audio Tape** for In the Barnyard: *I Love Animals* 💻 See the Houghton Mifflin **Internet** resources for additional activities
3 **Instruct** *and* **Integrate** *Pacing: 1-2 days*	**Reading/Listening Center,** Comprehension, T82 Phonics/Decoding, T83–T84 Concepts About Print, T85 Vocabulary, T86 Listening, T87 **Independent Reading & Writing,** T88–T89 **Language/Writing Center,** Oral Language, T90 Writing, T91 **Cross-Curricular Center,** Cross-Curricular Activities, T92–T93	**Challenge,** T82, T84, T92 **Extra Support,** T82, T83, T84, T85 **Students Acquiring English,** T90	**Poster** Doughy Animals, T91 **My Big Dictionary,** T83 **Letter, Word, and Picture Cards,** T82, T83, T87 *Literacy Activity Book* Comprehension, p. 75 Phonics/Decoding, pp. 77, 78 Vocabulary, p. 79 Tear-and-Take, pp. 81–82 📼 **Audio Tape** for In the Barnyard: *I Love Animals* 💻 See the Houghton Mifflin **Internet** resources for additional activities

✔ **Indicates Tested Skills.** *See page T11 for assessment options.*

1

Introduce *the* Literature

Shared Reading and Writing

Poster

I Love Little Pussy

I love little pussy,
Her coat is so warm,
And if I don't hurt her
She'll do me no harm.
So I'll not pull her tail,
Nor drive her away,
But pussy and I
Very gently will play.
She shall sit by my side,
And I'll give her some food;
And pussy will love me
Because I am good.

Literacy Activity Book, p. 73

INTERACTIVE LEARNING

Warm-up/Build Background

Sharing a Poem

- Before reading the poster "I Love Little Pussy," read just its title. Ask children what kind of animal the poem will talk about. Then show the poster and invite children to describe the little cats.

- Read the poem. Invite children to talk about animals they love and why.

Shared Reading

LAB, p. 72

Preview and Predict

- Display *I Love Animals*. Read aloud the title and the author's name. Explain that Flora McDonnell wrote the words *and* drew the pictures for the story.

- Discuss who "I" in the title refers to. Help children conclude that "I" refers to the young girl on the cover.

- Briefly discuss the cover illustration. Ask children to predict where this story takes place, and what kinds of animals the girl loves.

Read Together

- Invite children to read along with you to see if their predictions match the story.

- Read the selection through for enjoyment and comprehension. Point to the words as you read, using a sweeping motion across the page from left to right. Emphasize the animal names and their actions.

- Pause occasionally to allow children to look at the animal pictured on a spread and use picture clues to tell why the girl loves that animal.

Personal Response

Have children complete *Literacy Activity Book* page 73 to show which farm animal from the story they liked best. Children may like to use their pictures to tell family members about *I Love Animals*.

Shared Writing: *A Class Book*

Brainstorming   Ask children to draw pictures of animals they love. The animals can be farm animals or other animals children keep as pets. Have children write their names or initials on their drawings.

Drafting   Display children's pictures, and then ask each child to tell why he or she loves the animal. Record children's responses on chart paper. Encourage them to tell you how to spell one or two of the words, especially any words that name the animals. Write the child's initials after his/her sentence.

Publishing   Provide writing paper, and have each child copy from the chart the sentence that he or she has suggested. Bring children's drawings and sentences together to make a class book. Write *We Love Animals* on the cover, and invite children to draw illustrations for the cover. Add the book to your classroom library.

Choices for Rereading

You may want to use one or more of the choices for rereading suggested on page T80.

- Recognizing Language Patterns
- Acting It Out!
- Cooperative Reading

Interact *with* Literature

Reading Strategies

▶ **Evaluate**

Student Application Ask children if they have enjoyed the stories they have read in this theme. Have them talk about why it might be a good idea to read three stories about the same theme–barnyard animals.

Purpose Setting

Suggest that as children reread the story with you, they list in their Journals the animals that the girl loves. Children can draw and/or write as they make their lists. Point out that this will help them retell the story to their friends or families.

I love Jock, my dog.

6

I love the ducks

8

QuickREFERENCE

Home Connection

Invite children to briefly talk about their own well-loved pets. Who would they mention in place of Jock, the dog? Children may enjoy sharing photos or drawings of their own pets.

 Students Acquiring English

This story has good illustrations that support the vocabulary, and the pattern is easy to follow.

High-Frequency Words Review

Reread the sentence on page 6; then ask a volunteer to point to the word *my*. Repeat with *the* in the sentence on pages 8-9. Note that *the* appears twice in this sentence.

7

waddling to
the water.

Phonics/Decoding

Initial *d*

Teach/Model

Read aloud the sentence on page 6, pointing to the words as you say them. Frame *dog* and ask children to name the first letter. *(d)* Have children say *dog*, listening for the beginning sound. Conclude that *d* stands for /d/.

Display Magic Picture *dinosaur*.

Materials
• Picture Card: *dinosaur*

Explain that Magic Picture *dinosaur* can help children remember the sound for *d*. Have children say *dog* and *dinosaur*, listening for the beginning sound.

Practice/Apply

Reread pages 8-9. Then repeat the sentence, asking children to raise their hands when they hear a word that begins like *dog* and *dinosaur*. Frame the word *ducks* and have a volunteer point to the initial *d*.

SKILL FINDER *Decoding* D *Words*, page T83

MEETING INDIVIDUAL NEEDS **Extra Support**

Vocabulary Remind children that in *The Rain Puddle*, the pig waddled, or swayed from side to side as it moved. Invite a volunteer to demonstrate a duck's waddling.

Phonemic Awareness Review

Identifying Alliteratives
Reread the sentence on page 9 and ask a volunteer to identify the two words that begin with the same sound. *(waddling, water)*

Interact *with* Literature

BIG BOOK

I love the hens
hopping up
and down.

10

Reading Strategies

▶ **Think About Words**

Discuss how children might figure out the word *hens* on page 10.

The story says: *I love the ___hopping up and down.*

- **What makes sense** The sentence tells about something that hops. We have been reading about animals, so the word probably is the name of an animal that can hop.

- **Sounds for letters** Point to the word *hens*, noting that it begins with *h*.

- **Picture clues** The picture shows some birds hopping up and down. I know that hens are birds and the word *hens* begins with the sound for *h*. The word must be hens. Listen as I reread the sentence. Tell me if you think *hens* makes sense.

Have children reread the sentence with you to confirm that *hens* makes sense.

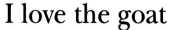
I love the goat

Quick**REFERENCE**

Phonemic Awareness Review

Identifying Alliteratives
Reread the sentence on page 10 and ask a volunteer to identify the two words that begin with the same sound. *(hens, hopping)*

Challenge

Antonyms Ask children to listen for words that are opposite in meaning as you reread the sentence on page 10. *(up, down)*

High-Frequency Words Review

Ask children to find the word *the* in the sentence on page 10. Ask them to find *the* two times in the sentence on pages 12-13.

11

racing across
the field.

MINILESSON

Phonics/Decoding

Initial *h*

Materials
● Picture Card: *horse*

Teach/Model

Display Magic Picture *horse*. Have children say *horse*, listening for the beginning sound. Reread the sentence on page 10. Invite volunteers to name the two words in this sentence that begin with the sound they hear at the beginning of *horse*. *(hens, hopping)*

Practice/Apply

Help children find other words in the story that begin with the sound for *h*. *(hee-haw, her)*

SKILL FINDER *Decoding* H *Words,* pages T45, T55

Extra Support

Vocabulary Invite volunteers to suggest a meaning for the word *racing*. Help them understand that *racing* in the sentence on pages 12–13 means to "move very quickly."

Interact
with
Literature

I love the donkey

16

QuickREFERENCE

Vocabulary

Help children understand that *braying* is a word that describes how a donkey makes noise. Demonstrate how to bray like a donkey. Then use your hand to show a *swishing* tail movement. Invite children to bray and then swish.

T72 *I Love Animals*

Big Book pp. 14, 16

braying
"hee-haw!"

15

I love the cow
swishing her tail.

17

MINILESSON

Concepts About Print

Last Letter in Written Words

Teach/Model

Remind children that they have learned how to find the first letter in a written word. Display page 17, and invite a volunteer to read the word *the* in the sentence. Point to the last letter in the word and have children name it. Demonstrate how to cover up the first two letters of *the* with your hand so you can see the *e* at the end of *the* more clearly.

Practice/Apply

Invite children to identify the last letter in each remaining word on page 17.

SKILL FINDER | *Word Find,* page T85

Interact *with* Literature

BIG BOOK

I love the pig with

Reading Strategies

▶ **Predict/Infer Evaluate**

Student Application Point out the numbered tag on the mother pig. Ask children why they think the pig has the tag. (to help the farmer keep track of his animals) **Have** them consider what would happen if you gave them numbers in the classroom instead of using their names. Would that be a good idea?

Then to elicit how children feel about what they are reading, ask:

• Is it fun to read about more and more animals the girl loves? Why or why not? Shall we keep on reading?

I love the pony

20

QuickREFERENCE

Vocabulary

Ask children to point to each piglet on page 18. Help children understand that *piglets* are baby pigs. Ask children to find other baby animals in the story and talk about their special names. *(lamb, kittens)*

Phonemic Awareness Review

Identifying Alliteratives
Point out that the words *love* and *little* begin with the same sound. Ask children to name two other words in the sentence that begin with the same sound. *(pig, piglets)*

all her little piglets.

19

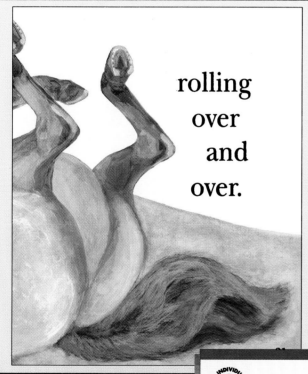

rolling
over
and
over.

Vocabulary

High Frequency Word: *I*

TESTED SKILL

Teach/Model

Reread the sentence on pages 18-19. Ask a volunteer to point to the first word in this sentence: *I.*

Display Word Card *I.*

Explain that the word *I* is spelled with just one letter: *I. I* is always written with a capital letter because it names a person. Review that the "I" in the story refers to the young girl, through whose eyes the author is telling the story.

Have volunteers find and frame the word *I* on page 17.

> **Materials**
> ● Word Card: *I*

Practice/Apply

Open to spreads in the selection at random. Invite volunteers to find, frame, and read the word *I* on each spread.

SKILL FINDER   *What I Love,* page T86

MEETING INDIVIDUAL NEEDS

Extra Support

Concepts Invite children to suggest reasons the pony would lie on his back and roll over and over. Explain that some animals do this to scratch their backs because they can't reach their backs any other way.

Interact
with
Literature

BIG BOOK

I love the sheep
bleating to
her lamb.

22

I love
the cat

24

QuickREFERENCE

Challenge

Ask children what kind of clothing
material we get from sheep. (wool)
Have children name some types of
wool clothing. (hat, jacket, sweater)

23

washing her kittens.

25

Phonics/Decoding

Phonogram -at

Teach/Model

Read aloud the sentence on pages 24-25, emphasizing the word *cat*. Print *cat* on the chalkboard. Ask children to say *cat* and listen for the sounds in the word.

Print *sat* below *cat*. Ask children how the words are the same. Point to *sat*, explaining that it has the same ending sounds as *cat*, but begins with the sound for *s*. Ask children to name the word. If necessary, tell them the word is *sat*.

Practice/Apply

Use Letter Cards to display the word *cat* on the chalkboard ledge. Place Letter Cards *s, m,* and *h* to the side of *cat*. Lead children to see they can remove the *c* in *cat* and replace it with one of the other letters to make a new word. Have children take turns making new words and reading them.

Materials
● Letter Cards: *c, a, t*

SKILL FINDER Phonogram -at *Riddles,* page T84

Health Link

Point out that the mother cat licks her kittens to keep them clean. Invite children to describe ways they keep themselves clean.

Science Link

Ask children if they have ever been licked by a cat. Invite them to describe how a cat's tongue feels. Explain that the roughness of a cat's tongue makes it easier for the cat to lick off dirt in its fur.

2

I Love Animals

THEME: IN THE BARNYARD

Interact *with* Literature

Reading Strategies

▶ **Evaluate**

Student Application Help children understand that the sentence on page 28 tells what this story is all about. Then ask them to decide whether the animals love the little girl back. Invite them to share the reasons for their decision. Encourage them to refer to the picture on pages 28-29 of the story.

Self-Assessment

Encourage children to think about their reading. Have them ask themselves:
- Were parts of the story confusing to me? What did I do to help myself understand better?
- Could I tell a friend what the most important things in this story are?

BIG BOOK

I love the turkey

26

I love all
the animals.

28

QuickREFERENCE

Vocabulary

Explain to children that *strutting* tells how the turkey walks. Demonstrate strutting and then invite volunteers to strut like a turkey, too.

Phonics/Decoding Review

Read the word *me* on page 29 as you point to it. Ask children to tell what letter the word begins with. (*m*) Have them listen to identify words that begin with /m/: *my, sun, house, mail, mouse.*

strutting
around
the yard.

27

I hope they love me.

Comprehension

Classify/ Categorize

Teach/Model

Explain to children that things that are alike can be grouped together. Ask them to look at the turkey on pages 22 and 23 and describe it as completely as possible. Elicit that a turkey has two legs. Help children find other animals in the story that also have two legs. (hens, ducks) Explain that you can call this group "animals that have two legs."

Compare the turkey to the cat on pages 20-21. Ask children to explain why the cat wouldn't belong in the group of animals that have two legs. Help children see that a cat has four legs.

Practice/Apply

Invite children to find other animals in the story that would belong in the group "Animals with four legs." (dog, goat, donkey, cow, pigs, pony, sheep)

SKILL FINDER

Feathers or Fur? page T82

Minilessons, Theme 1

2

Interact *with* Literature

Rereading

Choices for Rereading

Literacy Activity Book, p.74

> I love _____.
>
>
> I love _____.

Recognizing Language Patterns
LAB, p. 74

Help children identify the language pattern in the story:

I love the _____ _____.
        (animal name)   (action)

Invite children to brainstorm different animals and actions that could fill in the blanks. Then have children complete *Literacy Activity Book* page 74 by writing or dictating words to complete the story pattern. Have children draw pictures to accompany their writing.

Listen and Read

Audio Tape for In the Barnyard: *I Love Animals*

Extra Support Invite small groups to listen to the Audio Tape. Encourage them to follow along with a copy of the story and to chime in on the repetitive sentences.

Acting It Out!

To promote story comprehension, have children make a paper bag puppet for each story animal. Ask volunteers to use the puppets to act out what each animal does as you reread the story.

Materials
- one lunch-size paper bag for each story animal
- yarn, construction paper, crayons, and other crafts materials
- scissors, glue

Cooperative Reading

Distribute copies of the Little Big Book to partners. Have children reread or retell the story, using the pictures as prompts. After the initial spread, partners might take turns reading the first and second parts of each sentence. For example:

- I love the ducks *(Child #1 reads)*
- waddling to the water. *(Child #2 reads)*

Students Acquiring English Pair children acquiring English with strong English readers. Have the stronger reader read the part of Child #2.

Informal Assessment

- Use the Responding activities to assess children's general understanding of *I Love Animals.*
- As children reread or retell the story, note their ability to move from the front to the back of the book.

Responding

Choices for Responding

Story Talk

Talk with children in small groups about the following questions:

- Why does the girl only talk about farm animals? If she lived in the city, what kinds of animals do you think she might say she loved?

- What animals do you love? How might you show these animals that you love them?

Home Connection

Ask children to respond to the scene on pages 28-29. Ask if they would like to be the girl in the story. Why or why not?

Encourage children who would like to be the girl to take on that role as they retell the story to family members.

Can You Guess Who?

Invite children one at a time to choose a farm animal from the shoebox barn and to keep it hidden from classmates. Ask each child to describe the animal, being careful not to say its name, and to then role-play how the animal might show that it loves you. Other children can try to guess the animal.

Materials

- toy farm animals or pictures of farm animals

- a shoebox covered with paper to look like a barn

Portfolio Opportunity

- Save *Literacy Activity Book* page 74 as a record of children's ability to identify language patterns in the story.

- Children's drawings and writing can be placed in their portfolios as a record of their work.

Instruct
and
Integrate

Comprehension

Literacy Activity Book, p.75

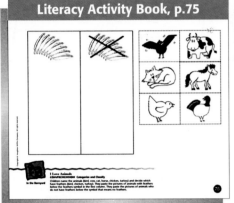

Practice Activities

Feathers or Fur?

LAB, p. 75

Extra Support On the chalkboard, list the story animals in a chart. Then have children look at the pictures in *I Love Animals* to decide if the animal has feathers or fur (or hair) on its body. Write *X* in the appropriate columns to show the animals' features.

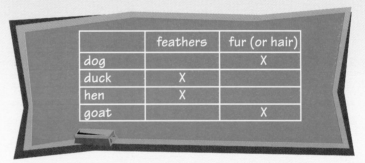

	feathers	fur (or hair)
dog		X
duck	X	
hen	X	
goat		X

Challenge Change the headings to house pets and farm animals, and erase the X's. Have children recategorize the animals. Have children complete *Literacy Activity Book* page 75.

Materials

Picture Cards:

Set #1—*pajamas, jeans, hat, belt, ring, necklace, jacket, mittens*

Set #2—*bed, desk, door, lamp, mailbox, garden, sink, table*

Set #3—*jam, banana, toaster, tomato, vegetables, sandwich, lemon, lettuce*

Set #4—*bike, bus, car, van, helicopter, jet, motorcycle, wagon*

Informal Assessment

As children complete the activities, note their ability to
- group like items and to name categories
- read and spell words with *d*

Picture-Card Sort

- Create four groups, giving each a set of Picture Cards.

- Have children work together to sort the cards into categories of their own choosing.

- Children need not use all cards, but a category must have at least two cards in it. Encourage group discussion!

When children have a category, they should raise their hands to show they are ready. Check children's work; then ask them to sort the cards *another* way.

Food Groupings

Have children cut out pictures of food and classify the pictures into two groups of their own choosing. To show the classifications, they can fold a piece of paper in half and paste the pictures from the two groups on either side of the fold. Invite children to share their classifications with the class. For example:

- foods that I like, foods that I don't

Materials

- old magazines and newspapers
- scissors
- construction paper
- paste or glue

Phonics/Decoding

Practice Activities

Literacy Activity Book, p.77

Decoding *d* Words

Display Picture Card *duck* along the chalkboard ledge. Above it, write the words *the duck.* Have children read the words. Point out that *duck* begins with the sound for *d*.

Ask children to imagine that this little duck can talk. He wants to tell about all the things he loves. Construct this sentence in a pocket chart:

"My ," said the duck.

Ask a volunteer to read the sentence. Ask if *doll* and *duck* begin with the same sound. Have children write the first letter in the word *doll.*

Continue the activity, substituting other Picture Cards for *doll.*

Materials

Picture Cards: *duck*
Word Cards: *the, said, my*
Punctuation Cards

What Does the Dog Love?

LAB, p. 77

Have children help the dog find his dog-house by identifying words that begin with d on *Literacy Activity Book* page 77.

Extra Support Some children may wish to complete the page with partners.

My Big Dictionary/ Spelling *d* Words

Display pages 12-13 of *My Big Dictionary.* Read *dig, dinosaur, dog,* and *dolphin,* pointing to the initial *d* and emphasizing the sound /d/ as you read. Then invite partners to work together to find things on page 13 that begin with the sound for *d*. You may want to encourage children to use temporary spellings and make a list of their words for their journals.

My Big Dictionary

Portfolio Opportunity

- Save *Literacy Activity Book* page 77 as a record of children's work on decoding words with *d*.

- Save the Food Groupings activity as a record of children's ability to classify.

3

Instruct *and* Integrate

Phonics/Decoding

Practice Activities

Phonogram -*at* Riddles

Extra Support Provide each child with a card for the phonogram -*at* and Letter Cards *h*, *s*, and *m*. Read the following riddles, and have children answer each one and then spell the answer word.

- I keep your head warm in winter.
  What am I? *(hat)*
- Today you sit in your chair.
  Yesterday you *(say "blank")* in your chair.
  What am I? *(sat)*
- You wipe your feet on me before coming into the house.
  What am I? *(mat)*

That Cat!

LAB, p. 78

Children practice forming words with the phonogram -*at* on *Literacy Activity Book* page 78.

Challenge Encourage children to create additional -*at* words using what they know about the sounds for other consonant letters.

Grow a Story with -*at*

Children will enjoy thinking of words to rhyme with cat. Have volunteers, one at a time, name a rhyming word. Join each word as it is suggested to cat in some way to "grow a story." For example:

Child 1: fat
Teacher: The fat cat
Child 2: hat
Teacher: The fat cat wearing a hat

Write the story as it grows right before children's eyes.

Informal Assessment

Note the ease with which children generate and read words with the phonogram -*at*. Use the Word Find activity to assess children's ability to identify the last letter of a written word.

Concepts About Print

Practice Activities

Word Find

Extra Support Invite pairs of children to go on a word find around the classroom. Each child in a pair takes turns finding a word in print and identifying its last letter. If the other child agrees with the identification, the pair gets one point. If the other child disagrees, the two must come to some consensus about which letter is last before getting a point. (You may wish to show children how to write hash marks to tally their points before beginning this activity.) Which pair has the most points?

Afterwards, talk with children about how the pairs resolved any disagreements.

A Lasting Picture

Provide children with old magazines and newspapers. Have them cut out individual words to use in the making of a word collage. Ask children to circle the last letter in each word they find. Then they can arrange their words in a design or pattern that can be decorated with odds and ends materials available in the classroom.

A Few More Words About Animals

Invite children to dictate sentences about some of the animals the girl in the story loves. Write the sentences as they are suggested. Then point to individual words within the sentences and have children circle the last letter in each.

Instruct *and* Integrate

Vocabulary

Literacy Activity Book, p. 79

Practice Activities

What *I* Love

LAB, p. 79

Introduce this activity by showing children examples of the rebus construction I _____ that is often used in ads, bumper stickers, and greeting cards. Or, write and draw a sample of this rebus:

I my  .

Ask a volunteer to read the sentence. Then have children use it as a model for writing their own sentences with I .

Have children complete *Literacy Activity Book* page 79.

Word Search

Divide the class into small groups to look through the Little Big Books to find the High-Frequency Words *I, the, said,* and *my.* Have each group tally the number of times they find each word. Ask all the groups to share their findings with the class. Which word was found most often?

Tear-and-Take Story

LAB, pp. 81-82

Have children remove *Literacy Activity Book* pages 81–82, fold it to make a book, and read the story.

Home Connection Suggest that children take the book home to read to their families.

The Hat

Informal Assessment

- As children complete the Vocabulary activities, note how readily they are able to identify the high-frequency words.
- Children's participation in and responses to the Listening activities will show how well they can recognize the beginning sound of a word.

Listening

Practice Activities

What Doesn't Belong?

Read aloud the following groups of words to children. Ask them to name the one word that doesn't belong and then tell how the remaining words are alike. If necessary, give children a hint. Tell them to listen carefully to the beginning sound in each word.

door	sun	hammer	mouse
doctor	sea	*nest*	*hat*
fire	*turkey*	house	milk
desk	sand	hippo	mop

Listening for Beginning Sounds

To reinforce initial sounds, give each child letter cards for *h* and *d*. Reread the story. Have children hold up the appropriate card when they hear a word that begins with the sound for that letter.

Materials
- Letters Cards: *h, d*

Listen and Read!

Audio Tape for In the Barnyard: *I Love Animals*

Set up copies of the Little Big Book along with the Audio Tape in a quiet corner of the room. Have children listen to the tape as they follow along in the books.

Portfolio Opportunity

Save children's word search papers as an example of children's ability to recognize high-frequency words.

3

Instruct *and* Integrate

Independent Reading & Writing

The Horse's Hat

The Horse's Hat
by Andrew Clements

This story provide practice and application for the following skills:

- **High-Frequency Words**: *I, the*
- **Phonics/Decoding Skills**: Initial *d* and *h*; phonogram *-at*
- **Cumulative Review**: Previously taught decoding skills and High-Frequency Words

Informal Assessment

- As children read aloud *The Horse's Hat* and complete other activities, note whether they begin to recognize the high-frequency words on sight.
- As children reread the story on their own, note whether they turn pages in sequence.
- As children complete the writing activities, assess their ability to use resources.

INTERACTIVE LEARNING

Independent Reading
Watch Me Read

Preview and Predict

- Display *The Horse's Hat*. Read aloud the title and the names of the author and illustrator.

- Briefly discuss the cover illustration. Have children identify the horse and it's new hat. Ask how they think the horse feels about the hat.

- Preview pages 1-5, encouraging children to comment on the pictures. Note the rebuses used in the sentences and identify them for children: *horse, goat, duck, chicken*.

- Ask children to name other barnyard animals that might appear in the story, suggesting *sheep* and *pig* if they do not. Then ask them to predict what will happen to the horse's hat.

Read the Story

- Have children read independently to find out if their predictions match what happens.

- After reading ask children: What happened to the horse's hat? Is this how you thought the story would end?

Rereading

- Ask children to tell what sounds a real horse, goat, duck, chicken, sheep, and pig make. Then invite them to reread the story, adding these sounds to the animal's lines. Children might say, for example, "Neigh! My Hat!" said the horse.

- Invite children to form groups of six to reread the story. Suggest that each child assume an animal role to read the story aloud. Encourage them to use their voices to show how the animals feel as they speak.

Responding

- Ask children how the horse feels about its ruined hat. Encourage them to draw and write about a time something of theirs was ruined.

Student-Selected Reading

Favorite Big Books

Encourage children to reread Big Books from previous themes. Children might read the books independently or with partners.

Books for Browsing

Display several of the book suggested in the Bibliography on pages T6-T7. You may want to give Book Talks for a few of these titles. Then invite children to read the books, or browse through them, during their leisure time. You might also schedule a special time for "Book Browsing" each day.

Student-Selected Writing

 ### Scrapbooks

Encourage children to make scrapbooks for the "In the Barnyard" theme. They can ask family members to help them find photographs and pictures to put into their scrapbooks. The books will provide a source of inspiration for children's writing.

 ### My Own Words

Suggest that children "collect" words they enjoy or use often in their writing. Children who especially enjoy the barnyard theme may want to make special "pictionaries" of animals and other things found on a farm.

Books for Independent Reading

Encourage children to choose their own books. They might choose one of the following titles.

The Horse's Hat
by Andrew Clements

Spots Feathers and Curly Tails
by Nancy Tafuri

I Love Animals
by Flora McDonnell

Have pairs of children share the reading of these. Some children may be able to read them independently.

See the theme Bibliography on pages T6-T7 for more theme-related books for independent reading.

Ideas for Independent Writing

Encourage children to write on self-selected topics. For those who need help getting started, suggest one of the following activities:

- an "I Love You" **note** to a pet
- an **invitation** to the theme celebration
- a **caption** for a farm picture

Portfolio Opportunity

Save examples of the writing children do independently on self-selected topics.

3

Instruct and Integrate

Oral Language

Choices for Oral Language

Mine's the Best!

Take a vote to see which animals children like best. Then ask each child to think about all the reasons he or she likes a certain animal best. Ask volunteers to come to the front of the room and try to convince the others that their animal is best.

Afterwards take another vote on favorite animals. Did any children change their minds? What did others say that made them change their minds?

Just for Fun

Children may enjoy trying some language play. Have them listen as you read some jokes related to animals and animal sounds. See if they can come up with the answers. Talk about each answer as it is revealed.

What is a duck's favorite snack? (QUACKers)

Who always wears shoes to bed? (horse)

Where would cows rather live? (on the MOO-n)

Where do sheep go for a haircut? (to the BAH-BAH shop)

Using Exact Action Words

 Students Acquiring English
Read aloud this sentence: *The duck is going.* Invite a volunteer to pretend to be a duck and go.

Then read this sentence: *The duck is waddling.* Ask another volunteer to pretend to be a duck and waddle.

Ask children to decide which word, *going* or *waddling*, gives a better picture of how the duck is moving. Then invite children to suggest other action words for *going* and to act them out.

Informal Assessment

- Use the activities on this page to informally assess children's ability to experiment with and enjoy words.

- As children complete the writing activities, note their use of correct directional patterns.

 # Writing

Choices for Writing

No-Bake Animal Cookies

Display and discuss the poster "Doughy Animals" with children. Then invite children to make their own doughy animals using your favorite salt dough recipe or the edible one at the right.

Have children use clean hands to mix together the cream cheese and graham cracker crumbs. Then children can form the resulting dough into animal shapes and decorate them.

Children can package their cookies in the sandwich bags and create labels for the cookies with a product name and a list of ingredients. Afterward, children can write a group recipe for their cookies, copy it, and bring it home to make with their families.

Materials

Ingredients per child:

- 4 oz. cream cheese
- 4 graham cracker squares, crushed
- 1 sandwich bag with twist tie
- sprinkles, cocoa powder, small candies, and other edible "decorations"

Poster

Describing

Invite each child to pick an animal from the selection and describe it as completely as possible. Tape-record children's descriptions. Encourage them to tell

- what the animal looks like,
- what kinds of sounds it makes,
- what it feels like when you pet it,
- what it smells like,
- how it moves when it walks, runs, or flies.

Other children can listen to the tape and draw pictures and write captions based on the descriptions.

Come to the Country Fair!

Provide children with red construction paper cutouts of a barn. Tell children they are going to write special invitations for people to come to their Country Fair, which celebrates the conclusion of this theme. Talk about the information needed in the invitation, and help children write the day, time, and place of the celebration on one side of the cutout. They can decorate the flip side with barnyard animals standing in front of the barn.

Portfolio Opportunity

Invite children to choose one of the written works from these activities to include in their portfolios.

Instruct
and
Integrate

Cross-Curricular Activities

Math

Barnyard Patterns

Make 2"x 2" cards with simple outline drawings of farm animals so that there are at least four cards that show each animal. Have children work in pairs and take turns. One child uses cards to create a patterned series. The other child figures out the pattern and adds the next picture in the series.

Challenge Invite children to create an oral pattern. Have one child choose two animals and create an ABAB pattern. (horse, cow, horse, cow) Ask another child to guess which animal will be next in the series.

Social Studies

Where Does Our Food Come From?

Discuss food products that come from the farm. Can children identify what the dairy products are all made from?

Have children bring in clean containers from dairy products and look at the ingredients. Help them find the word *milk* or *cream* on the labels. Point out that some foods are processed in factories before they come to the supermarket. To make ice cream, for example, milk and cream are combined with other ingredients and frozen at an ice cream factory.

Children can use the containers to create their own dairy cases in the dramatic play center. Have them affix price labels to their containers.

Materials
- empty, clean dairy product containers
- self-sticking notes

Music/Movement

Sounds of the Animals

If possible, play a recording of a piece of classical music, such as:

- *Carnival of the Animals* by Camille Sans-Saëns (PHILIPS: with André Previn conducting the Pittsburgh Symphony Orchestra)

- *Peter and the Wolf* by Sergei Prokofiev (VIRGIN)

Invite children to listen for the "sounds" of the animals; then encourage them to move creatively as they listen to the music a second time.

Science

Hay You!

Place a bale of hay in the science center. Encourage children to observe the hay in a variety of ways: with magnifying glasses, by lifting it as a group to compare its weight to other objects in the room, by lying on it to see what it would be like to sleep on, and so on. Invite children to record all their observations in words and/or drawings. Afterward, have children use the hay to make a scarecrow.

Theme Assessment Wrap-Up

Reflecting/Self-Assessment

Copy the chart below to distribute to children. Ask them which stories in the theme they liked best. Then discuss what was easy for them and what was more difficult as they read the selections and completed the activities. Have children put a check mark under either *Easy* or *Hard*.

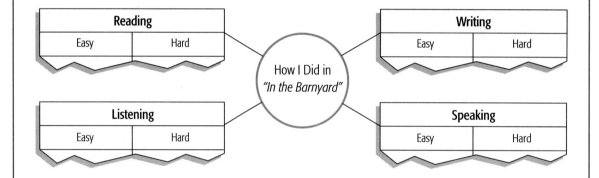

Reading	
Easy	Hard

Writing	
Easy	Hard

How I Did in "In the Barnyard"

Listening	
Easy	Hard

Speaking	
Easy	Hard

Monitoring Literacy Development

There will be many opportunities to observe and evaluate children's literacy development. As children participate in literacy activities, note whether each child has a beginning, a developing, or a proficient understanding of reading, writing and language concepts. The Observation Checklists, which can be used for recording and evaluating this information, appear in the *Teacher's Assessment Handbook*, and include

Concepts About Print and Book Handling Behaviors
• Concepts about print
• Book handling

Emergent Reading Behaviors
• Responding to literature
• Storybook rereading
• Decoding strategies

Emergent Writing Behaviors
• Writing
• Stages of Temporary Spelling

Oral Language Behaviors
• Listening attentively
• Listening for information
• Listening to directions
• Listening to books
• Speaking/language development
• Participating in conversations and discussions

Retelling Behaviors
• Retelling a story
• Retelling information text

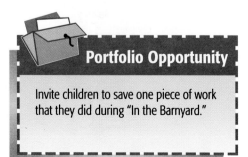

Portfolio Opportunity

Invite children to save one piece of work that they did during "In the Barnyard."

Choices for Assessment

Informal Assessment

Review the Observation Checklists and observation notes to determine the following:

- Did children's responses during and after reading indicate comprehension of the selections?

- How well did children understand the skills presented in this theme? Which skills should be reviewed and practiced in the next theme?

- Did children enjoy the cooperative activities related to the major theme concept?

Formal Assessment

Select formal tests that meet your classroom needs:

- *Kindergarten Literacy Survey*
- Theme Skills Test for "In the Barnyard"

See the *Teacher's Assessment Handbook* for guidelines for administering test and using answer keys and children's sample papers.

Portfolio Assessment

Evaluating Progress in Emergent Writing

Emergent writers need many opportunities to experiment with writing. Kindergarten children enjoy keeping and sharing journals as well as writing captions for their drawings and stories. At the beginning of school, demonstrate for children all the different ways kindergarten children can write—drawings, scribble writing, individual letters, words, sentences. Encourage them to write in any form.

Look for student progress in using writing to communicate; in understanding concepts of letters, words, and sentences; and in stages of temporary spelling. Use the Emergent Writing checklist to record your observations.

For more information on this and other topics, see the *Teacher's Assessment Handbook*.

Celebrating the Theme

Choices for Celebrating

A County Fair

Children can share some of the things they have done during this theme with family members and friends at a County Fair. To help children get ready, suggest that they

- distribute their farm motif invitations.

- help you make an additional batch of No-Bake Animal Cookies to serve, along with milk, as a snack.

On the big day, children, each wearing a blue ribbon pre-made by you, can

- take visitors on a "tour" of their miniature farm.

- re-enact favorite stories, or read aloud from one of the Big Books.

- share stories and books made by the class.

- demonstrate how to make butter.

See the Houghton Mifflin **Internet** resources for theme-related activities.

Theme Talk

Encourage children to share what they have learned during the theme.

- Talk about the books, poems, and songs they have read and sung.

- Review the high-frequency words *I* and *the.* Have children identify animal characters in the stories they've read whose names begin with the sounds for *h* and for *d.*

- Invite children to share favorite projects and writing activities.

Our Own Little Farm

Provide time for children to complete their miniature farm. They may want to make labels for various items on the farm. Or, they can create a "Key" similar to the one on the poster "Farm Places."

Self-Assessment

Have children ask themselves

- What have I learned about barnyards and farm animals that I didn't know before?

Nighttime

Table of Contents
THEME: Nighttime

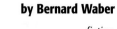

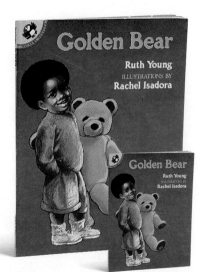

Big Books *LITERATURE FOR WHOLE CLASS AND SMALL GROUP INSTRUCTION*

by Nicki Weiss

fiction

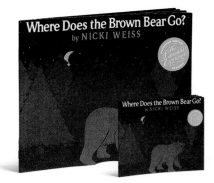

WATCH ME READ Books *PRACTICE FOR HIGH-FREQUENCY WORDS AND PHONICS SKILLS*

by Lauren Blass
illustrated by Tricia Santry

Each title is also available in black and white.
This version includes a home activity.

Bibliography

Books for the Library Corner

 Multicultural

 Science/Health

 Math

 Social Studies

 Music

 Art

Asleep, Asleep
by Mirra Ginsburg
Greenwillow 1992 (24p)
A mother helps her child fall asleep.

K Is for Kiss Goodnight: A Bedtime Alphabet
 by Jill Sardegna
Doubleday 1994 (32p)
Letters of the alphabet present a child's bedtime rituals.

Goodnight, Gorilla
by Peggy Rathmann
Putnam 1994 (32p)
Zoo animals follow the unsuspecting zookeeper home one night.

Moonlight
by Jan Ormerod
Lothrop 1982 (24p)
A girl's parents get sleepy as they try to put their daughter to bed. (Wordless)

Light
by Donald Crews
Greenwillow 1981 (32p)
A visual presentation of the types of light that shine in the night sky.

Sleepy Kittens
by Jill and Martin Leman
Tambourine 1993
Three kittens sleep everywhere but in their own bed.

The Midnight Circus
by Peter Collington
Knopf 1992 (32p)
A boy dreams he is the star of a circus. (Wordless)

Shhhh
by Kevin Henkes
Greenwillow 1989 (24p)
A girl wakes up her sleeping family.

Books for Teacher Read Aloud

Aunt Nina, Good Night
by Franz Brandenberg
Greenwillow 1989 (32p)
Aunt Nina invites her nieces and nephews to spend the night.

Moondance
by Frank Asch
Scholastic 1993 (32p)
Bear's wish to dance with the moon finally comes true.

Darkness and the Butterfly
 *by Ann Grifalconi*
Little 1987 (32p)
A small African girl is afraid of the dark.

Cat, Mouse and Moon
by Roxanne Dyer Powell
Houghton 1994 (32p)
A cat stalks a mouse in the moonlight.

Coyote Places the Stars
by Harriet Peck Taylor
Bradbury 1993 (24p)
Coyote arranges the stars in the shapes of his friends.

Dreams
 by Ezra Jack Keats
Macmillan 1974 (32p)
also paper
When Roberto can't sleep he watches a cat play in the night.

The Big Big Sea
by Martin Waddell
Candlewick 1994 (32p)
A child and her mother take a moonlit walk along the beach one night.

Half a Moon and One Whole Star
 by Crescent Dragonwagon
Macmillan 1986 (32p)
Aladdin 1990 paper
As Susan sleeps, nighttime comes to life around her.

How Many Stars in the Sky?
 by Lenny Holt
Tambourine 1991 (32p)
A father and son count the stars in the sky when they can't sleep.

Night Is Coming
by W. Nikola-Lisa
Dutton 1991 (32p)
A grandfather and granddaughter quietly watch night descend on their farm.

The Night Ones
 by Patricia Grossman
Harcourt 1991 (32p)
A bus carries four people to their nighttime jobs in the city.

Northern Lullaby
 by Nancy White Carlstrom
Philomel 1992 (24p)
An Alaskan child says goodnight to the inhabitants of the natural world around him.

One Snowy Night
by Nick Butterworth
Little 1989 (24p)
Percy, a park keeper, shares his home with many animals on a snowy night.

Peeping and Sleeping
 by Fran Manushkin
Clarion 1994 (32p)
Barry's father takes him out one night to see what is making a peeping sound.

Still As a Star: A Book of Nighttime Poems
selected by Lee Bennett Hopkins
Little 1989 (32p)
Fourteen poems about nighttime by well-known authors.

Bedtime for Frances
by Russell Hoban
Harper 1960 (32p) also paper
Frances the badger finds innumerable ways to put off going to bed.

All Night Near the Water

by Jim Arnosky
Putnam 1994 (32p)
Twelve newly hatched ducklings spend their first night on the lake with their mother.

When Sheep Cannot Sleep
by Satoshi Kitamura
Farrar 1986 (32p) also paper
A sleepless sheep takes a walk in the night.
Available in Spanish as *Cuando los borregos no pueden dormir.*

Books for Shared Reading

City Night
by Eve Rice
Greenwillow 1987 (24p)
Images and sounds of a city at night.

Do Not Disturb
by Nancy Tafuri
Greenwillow 1987 (32p)
Nighttime sounds keep a family on a camping trip from sleeping.

Going to Sleep on the Farm
by Wendy Cheyette Lewison
Dial 1992 (24p)
A father tells his son how animals go to sleep on a farm.

Goodnight Moon
by Margaret Wise Brown
Harper 1947 (32p) also paper
A bunny says goodnight to all of the objects in his room.
Available in Spanish as *Buenas Noches Luna.*

In the Still of the Night
by Jennifer Selby
Simon 1994 (24p)
A rowdy rooster wakes other animals and they all disturb the quiet night.

Twinkle, Twinkle, Little Star
by Iza Trapani
Whispering Coyote Press 1994 (32p)
A girl wishes upon a star in this extended version of the classic bedtime rhyme.

Midnight Pillow Fight
by Jan Omerod
Candlewick 1993 (24p)
Late one night Molly awakes and plays with pillows all around the house.

Sleepy ABC
by Margaret Wise Brown
Harper 1994 (32p)
Rhymes illustrate bedtime scenes for each letter of the alphabet.

Ten Sleepy Sheep

by Holly Keller
Greenwillow 1983 (32p)
A boy tries to count sheep to fall asleep, but their noise keeps him awake.

Night Rabbits
by Monica Wellington
Dutton 1995 (32p)
Two rabbits have a series of nighttime adventures.

This Is the Bear and the Scary Night
by Sarah Hayes
Little 1992 (24p)
A stuffed bear left in the park spends a scary night alone.

Time for Bed
by Mem Fox
Harcourt 1993 (32p)
Animals and humans get their children ready for bed.

Technology Resources

Computer Resources

Internet See the Houghton Mifflin Internet resources for additional bibliographic entries and theme-related activities.

Video Cassettes

Ira Sleeps Over *by Bernard Waber.* Listening Library
Happy Birthday, Moon *by Frank Asch.* Weston Woods
A Dark, Dark Tale *by Ruth Brown.* Weston Woods
Animals at Night Filmic Archives

Audio Cassettes

What's Under My Bed? *by James Stevenson.* Spoken Arts
Goodnight Moon *by Margaret Wise Brown.* Live Oak Media
Bedtime for Frances *by Russell Hoban.* Listening Library
Ten, Nine, Eight *by Molly Bang.* Am. Sch. Pub.

Filmstrips

Squawk to the Moon, Little Goose *by Edna Mitchell Preston.* Live Oak Media
AV addresses are in Teacher's Handbook, *pages H14–H15.*

Theme at a Glance

Reading/Listening Center

Selections	Comprehension Skills and Strategies	Phonemic Awareness	Phonics/Decoding	Concepts About Print
Ira Sleeps Over	✔ Story structure: character, T113 Understanding story characters, T126 Characters in other stories, T126 Similarities between characters in the story and readers' friends and family, T126 Reading strategies, T112, T114, T116, T118, T120, T122 **Rereading and responding**, T124–T125	✔ Produces alliteratives, T119 Naming animals, T127 Matching rhyming picture cards, T127 Recognizing rhymes, T127		
Golden Bear	✔ Fantasy/Realism, T143 Fantasy and realism in *Golden Bear*, T152 Using imagination, T152 Playing a real and make-believe game, T152 Reading strategies, T136, T138, T140, T142, T144, T146, T148 **Rereading and responding**, T150–T151		✔ Initial *b*, T139 ✔ Phonogram -*ug*, T141 Reading *b* words, T153 Finding *b* words, T153 Initial consonant game, T153 Spelling words with -*ug*, T154 Reading -*ug* words, T154	✔ Directionality: words, T145, T154 Left to right directionality to read words, T155 First letter of a word, T155
Where Does the Brown Bear Go?	✔ Noting details, T171 Noting details about characters and settings, T180 Noting details about characters, T180 Settings in other stories, T180 Setting pictures, T180 Reading strategies, T166, T168, T170, T172, T174, T176 **Rereading and responding**, T178–T179		✔ Initial *g*, T167 Initial *h*, T177 Naming *g* words, T181 Finding where the pictures go, T181 Spelling *g* and *b* words, T182 Mix-and-match letter sounds, T182 Playing word memory, T182 *G* name game, T182	✔ Recognizing two words that are alike, T173 Recognizing words that are alike, T183 Searching for words, T183 First and last letter, T183

✔ *Indicates Tested Skills. See page T105 for assessment options.*

A child's view of nighttime and going to bed

This theme is designed to take 2½ to 3 weeks, depending on your students' needs and interests.

This theme can be used in conjunction with themes found in another grade level.
Grade 1: The World Outside My Door

Writing/Language Center

Cross-Curricular Center

Vocabulary	Listening	Oral Language	Writing	Content Areas
		Acting out feelings, T128 Different kinds of stories, T128 Bedtime rituals, T128 Planning a sleep over, T128	Picture postcards, T129 Sharing special things, T129 New endings, T129	**Science:** investigating with a magnifying glass, T130 **Math:** sorting, T130 **Social Studies:** different kinds of homes, T131 **Art:** making sponge prints, T131
✓ High-frequency word: *have*, T137 Reading high-frequency words, T156 Finding hidden words, T156 Playing a word game, T156	Bedtime rhymes, T157 Telephone skills, T157	Rhyming language patterns, T158 Names for musical instruments, T158 Wishing on a star, T158	Class poem, T135 Writing wishes on a star, T159 Nighttime pictures, T159 Pictures of signs, T159	**Science:** learning about stars, T160 **Art:** making cloud picture, T160; making night lights, T161 **Music:** singing nighttime songs, T161
✓ High-frequency word: *go*, T169 ✓ High-frequency word: *a*, T175 Reading *a* and *go* sentences, T184 Playing a high-frequency word game, T184 Playing *a* and *go* tic-tac-toe, T184	Role-playing characters, T185 Listening for assignments, T185 Listening for rhyming words, T185	Setting the scene, T188 Telling a nighttime story, T188 Animals during the day, T188	Class story, T165 Best things about nighttime, T187 Self-selected topic, T187 Book based on the story, T189 Invitations, T189 Name tags, T189	**Social Studies:** day and night around the world, T190 **Science:** where real animals sleep, T190 **Art:** making a teddy bear picture frame, T191 **Health/Nutrition:** making peanut butter clay, T191

Meeting Individual Needs

Managing Instruction

Self-Selected Writing/ Journal Writing

Show emerging writers how to express their ideas while you are working with others and independent work will go more smoothly.

- Draw a picture of what you want to say.
- Write down the sounds you hear.
- Find words and letters in magazines.
- Draw a line where the word(s) can go later.
- Ask a friend.
- Scribble write.

You can then circulate periodically and each day take dictation on the front or back of a few children's writing.

For further information on this and other Managing Instruction topics, see the *Professional Development Handbook*.

Performance Standards

During this theme, children will

- *explore nighttime and going to bed*
- *make predictions and inferences*
- *retell or summarize and evaluate each selection*
- *apply comprehension skills: Story Structure (Beginning, Middle, End), Fantasy/Realism, Noting Details*
- *produce alliteratives and identify words beginning with the sounds for g and h*
- *recognize words with the phonogram -ug*
- *recognize the high-frequency words* have, go, *and* a
- *apply left-to-right directionality*
- *write a story*

Students Acquiring English	Challenge	Extra Support
• **Develop Key Concepts** Children focus on Key Concepts through a guessing game, playing word and letter games, and making charts.	• **Apply Critical Thinking** Children apply critical thinking by understanding story structure, distinguishing between fantasy and realism, and noting details.	• **Enhance Self-Confidence** With extra support provided for reading and responding to the literature, children will see themselves as active members of the reading community.
• **Expand Vocabulary** Children use context and picture clues, work with story props, discuss meanings, and model definitions. Children learn names for musical instruments, idioms, synonyms, and describing words.	• **Explore Topics of Interest** Activities that motivate further exploration include sharing nighttime songs, discussing phases of the moon, finding out what animals do at night, and learning about constellations.	• **Receive Increased Instructional Time on Skills** Practice activities in the Reading/Listening Center provide support with fantasy and reality, understanding characters, and recalling story details.
• **Act as a Resource** Children are asked to share their experiences with pets, dolls, musical instruments, family customs and bedtime rituals, and the names of animals in their native language.	• **Engage in Creative Thinking** Opportunities for creative expression include making postcards, creating an oral story about night scenes, making night lights, pantomiming, and writing a story.	• **Provide Independent Reading** Children can take home the Tear-and-Take stories in their *Literacy Activity Books* and the black-and-white versions of the WATCH ME READ titles to read.

Additional Resources

Invitaciones

Develop bi-literacy with this integrated reading/language arts program in Spanish. Provides authentic literature and real-world resources from Spanish-speaking cultures.

Language Support

Translations of Big Books in Chinese, Hmong, Khmer, and Vietnamese. *Teacher's Booklet* provides instructional support in English.

Students Acquiring English Handbook

Guidelines, strategies, and additional instruction for students acquiring English.

Planning for Assessment

Informal Assessment

Observation Checklist

- Concepts About Print/Book Handling
- Responding to Literature and Decoding Behaviors and Strategies
- Writing Behaviors and Stages of Temporary Spelling
- Listening and Speaking Behaviors
- Story Retelling and Rereading

Literacy Activity Book

Recommended pages for students' portfolios:
- Identify Alliteratives, p. 85
- Personal Response, p. 87
- Comprehension: Fantasy and Realism, p. 89
- Language Patterns, p. 96
- Phonics: Letter *g*, p. 99

Retellings—Oral/Written

- *Teacher's Assessment Handbook*

Formal Assessment

Kindergarten Literacy Survey

Evaluates children's literacy development. Provides holistic indicator of children's ability with
- Shared Reading/ Constructing Meaning
- Concepts About Print
- Phonemic Awareness
- Emergent Writing

Integrated Theme Test

- General Comprehension
- Phonics/Decoding
- Writing

Theme Skills Test

- Fantasy and Realism
- Letter Sounds *b* and *g*
- Phonogram *-ug*
- High-Frequency Words: *have, go, a*

Managing Assessment

Keeping Anecdotal Notes

Question: How can I keep anecdotal notes?

Answer: Anecdotal notes are useful to help you document learning that is hard to see in children's written work. For example, informal observational notes can record children's interests and their specific strengths and needs, and notes on oral reading can document reading fluency and word identification strategies.

Try these tips for keeping anecdotal notes:

- Keep a sheet of peel-off mailing labels on a clip board. When you want to record an anecdotal note, jot down the date, child's name, and notes on a label. Later, you can stick the labels onto individual pages for each child. That way, each child has a separate sheet but your note taking is kept simple.

- For specific areas such as retellings or oral language, use the observation checklists in the *Teacher's Assessment Handbook* to record your observations. The checklist may help you streamline your note taking.

- Keep notes during your conferences with individual children. This will ensure that you have an accurate record of your assessment. You may decide to share your notes with children, making them a part of the assessment process.

For more information on this and other topics, see the *Teacher's Assessment Handbook.*

Portfolio Assessment

The portfolio icon signals portfolio opportunities throughout the theme.

Additional Portfolio Tips:
- Evaluating Progress in Emergent Reading, T193

Launching the Theme

See the Houghton Mifflin **Internet** resources for additional activities.

Song Tape for Nighttime: "Twinkle, Twinkle, Little Star"

INTERACTIVE LEARNING

Warm-up

Singing the Theme Song

- Invite children who know "Twinkle, Twinkle, Little Star" to sing along as you play the tape. (See Teacher's Handbook, page H13.)

- Ask children to tell how night is different from day. Expand the discussion by asking: how children feel at night; where they go when night comes; and which nighttime cuddly objects they have.

Interactive Bulletin Board

Nighttime Cover a bulletin board with black construction paper.

- Distribute scissors, tag board, and aluminum foil, and show children how to make their own twinkling stars and crescent moon.

- Encourage children to sing the theme song with you as they place their stars and moon on the bulletin board to create a nighttime sky.

- Children can add to and change the bulletin board throughout the theme to display various Nighttime projects.

Ongoing Project

See the *Home/Community Connections Booklet* for theme-related materials.

A Class Sleep-Over Party

Plan with children a make believe sleep-over party to be held during the school day. Have them name activities they might enjoy at a sleep-over party and things they might want to bring. Ideas for planning the party include:

- Decorate the room with stars and nighttime sights, including a moon. Display the theme posters and projects.

- Invite the librarian, principal, or a parent to read bedtime stories.

- Prepare snacks using star and moon cookie cutters.

- Have children plan to bring in favorite cuddly toys.

Portfolio Opportunity

The Portfolio Opportunity icon highlights portfolio opportunities throughout the theme.

Choices for Centers

Creating Centers

Use these activities to create learning centers in the classroom.

Reading/Listening Center

- Story Characters and Me, T126
- "B's" for Golden Bear, T153
- Setting Pictures, T180

Language/Writing Center

- Picture Postcards, T129
- Star Wishes, T159
- *Where Do They Go?* Stories, T189

Cross-Curricular Center

- Science: Under Glass, T130
- Music: Night Music, T161
- Art: Brown Bear Keepsakes, T191

READ ALOUD

SELECTION:

Ira Sleeps Over

by Bernard Waber

Other Books by Bernard Waber

An Anteater Named Arthur

Lyle, Lyle Crocodile

Ira Says Goodbye

- **Child Study Children's Book Award**
- **Best Books for Children**
- **Children's Book Showcase**

Selection Summary

Ira is so happy! He is going to a sleep over at Reggie's house. But when Ira's sister asks if he is taking his teddy bear along, his happiness turns to worry. He has never slept without his teddy bear. Eventually, Ira decides to leave it home. But when Reggie quietly brings out his own stuffed bear, Ira goes home to get his.

Lesson Planning Guide

	Skill/Strategy Instruction	Meeting Individual Needs	Lesson Resources
1 Introduce *the* Literature *Pacing: 1 day*	**Preparing to Listen and Write** Warm-up/Build Background, T110 Read Aloud, T110	**Choices for Rereading,** T111 **Students Acquiring English,** T111	**Poster** Night Comes, T110 *Literacy Activity Book* Personal Response, p. 83
2 Interact *with* Literature *Pacing: 1-2 days*	**Reading Strategies** Predict/Infer, T112 Evaluate, T114, T120 Think About Words, T116 Summarize, T118, T122 **Minilessons** ✓ Story Structure: Character, T113 ✓ Produces Alliteratives, T119	**Students Acquiring English,** T112, T115, T118 **Extra Support,** T113, T116, T122, T124 **Challenge,** T119, T121 **Rereading and Responding,** T124–T125	**Story Props,** T125, H4 See the Houghton Mifflin **Internet** resources for additional activities.
3 Instruct *and* Integrate *Pacing: 1-2 days*	**Reading/Listening Center,** Comprehension, T126 Phonemic Awareness, T127 **Language/Writing Center,** Oral Language, T128 Writing, T129 **Cross-Curricular Center,** Cross-Curricular Activities, T130–T131	**Extra Support,** T126, T127, T130 **Students Acquiring English,** T127, T129 **Challenge,** T128, T129	**Poster** Bedtime, T128 **Letter, Word, and Picture Cards,** T127 *Literacy Activity Book* Comprehension, p. 84 Phonemic Awareness, p. 85 See the Houghton Mifflin **Internet** resources for additional activities.

✓ *Indicates Tested Skills. See page T105 for assessment options.*

Introduce *the* Literature

Preparing to Listen and Write

Poster

Literacy Activity Book, p. 83

Warm-up/Build Background

Sharing a Poem

- Display the poster "Night Comes . . . "

- Invite children to close their eyes and listen as you read it aloud.

- Ask them to tell what the poem is about and how it makes them feel. Invite children to tell some things that can make them feel less afraid at night, such as a night light or a favorite cuddly toy.

- Then read the poem again, encouraging children to join in.

Read Aloud

LAB, p. 83

Preview and Predict

- Display *Ira Sleeps Over*. Point to and read aloud the title and the author/illustrator's name.

- Have children identify Ira and his teddy bear on the cover. Invite them to comment on what Ira is wearing and where he might be going.

- Recall *Ten in a Bed*, in which ten children had a *sleep over*. Have children explain what it means to *sleep over*.

- Read aloud pages 3-7 of the story. Ask children to predict what Ira's problem is and what he might do about it.

Read

Invite children to listen as you read *Ira Sleeps Over*. Consider using "different voices" to help children recognize who is speaking and to maintain the story's friendly, conversational tone. As you read, stop now and then for children to check and/or revise their predictions.

Personal Response

Home Connection Have children complete *Literacy Activity Book* page 83 to show what they would like to do if they slept over at a friend's house. Encourage children to take the page home to share with their families.

Story Dialogue

Students Acquiring English As you read the characters' dialogue, exaggerate the inflection and tone of voice to help convey meaning. Promote children's oral language skills by pausing now and then for children to repeat the dialogue after you. Encourage them to experiment with how the words are spoken. You might have children try, for example, saying good night in a variety of ways. (in a nice friendly way, in a teasing way, as a question, and as if you were angry)

How Ira Feels

Pause after reading pages 8, 11, 15, 19, 25, 28, 33, and 45. Have children use story clues and picture clues to tell how they think Ira feels at these points in the story. Encourage them to tell how they might feel in the same situation.

Evaluating Ira's Decision

Invite children to evaluate what they think of Ira's decision either to take or not to take his teddy bear to Reggie's house. Throughout the story, whenever you read about Ira's decision to take or leave his teddy bear, have them stand if they agree with what Ira decides. Ask those standing why they agree with what Ira decides.

More Choices for Rereading Aloud

Choose one or more of the activities suggested on page T124.

- Changing His Mind?
- Dramatize the Story
- Independent Storytime

2

Interact *with* Literature

READ ALOUD

I was invited to sleep at Reggie's house.

Was I happy!

I had never slept at a friend's house before.

3

But I had a problem.
It began when my sister said:

"Are you taking your teddy bear along?"

"Taking my teddy bear along!" I said.
"To my friend's house? Are you kidding?
That's the silliest thing I ever heard!
Of course, I'm not taking my teddy bear."

4   5

Reading Strategies

▶ **Predict/Infer**

Teacher Modeling Tell children that to help them enjoy and understand a story good readers think about the things that happen and try to guess what will happen next in a story.

Think Aloud

Ira was so happy he was going to sleep at Reggie's house – until his sister mentioned his teddy bear.

I bet he thought, "It would be fun to sleep at a friend's house, but I wonder – How would I feel sleeping in a different place? What would that place be like at night?"

Now I think I understand Ira's problem and why he kept changing his mind about taking his teddy bear.

Purpose Setting

Invite children to listen as you read the story again. Encourage them to think about things that keep making Ira change his mind about taking his teddy bear.

Quick**REFERENCE**

Students Acquiring English

Idioms If children are confused by the phrase *"To my friend's house?"* explain that it is a continuation of Ira's response *"Taking my teddy bear along!"* and that *kidding* means *joking* or *fooling around.*

Journal

Ask children to draw a picture to show how Ira feels about going to Reggie's house to sleep over. Encourage them to draw or write about how they would feel if they were Ira.

And then she said:

"But you never slept without your teddy bear before. How will you feel sleeping without your teddy bear for the very first time? Hmmmmmmm?"

6   7

"I'll feel fine.
I'll feel great.
I will probably love sleeping without my teddy bear.
Just don't worry about it," I said.

"Who's worried?" she said.

9

 Extra Support

Reread the questions Ira's sister asks on page 7. Note that *Hmmmmmm?* is another way of asking a question a second time, when the person you have asked doesn't answer your question the first time you ask it.

MINILESSON

Comprehension
Story Structure: Character

TESTED SKILL

Teach/Model

Ask children to name the most important character in the story. Invite them to tell what they know about Ira. Explain that by thinking about the things Ira says and does, they can figure out what kind of a person he is. Model how children might think about the main character, Ira.

Think Aloud

I think Ira cares about what other people think. He listens to what his sister says and worries about what Reggie will think of him with a teddy bear. Like a lot of people, Ira doesn't want his friends to think he's a baby.

Practice/Apply

Help children make additional judgments about Ira. Ask:

- Do you think Ira would make a good friend?

- What does Ira do or say to make you think this?

SKILL FINDER
Understanding Story Characters, page T126

Minilessons, Themes 9 and 12

2

Interact with Literature

READ ALOUD

Reading Strategies

▶ **Evaluate**

Teacher Modeling Remind children that good readers think about what is happening in a story and why characters do certain things. Ask children to tell what Ira does after he realizes he has a problem. (asks his parents and sister for advice) Help children think about Ira's decision, by asking:

- Why does Ira ask his parents whether he should take his teddy bear? Do you think it was a good idea for him to ask his parents?

- What do you think of his sister's advice? Do you think it was a good idea for him to listen to her? (Perhaps he felt that since she is closer to his age, she would know something that his parents wouldn't.)

QuickREFERENCE

Music Link

Point out the bass (fiddle) on pages 12–13 and the piano on page 14. Invite children to tell what they know about these instruments. Encourage them to talk about musical instruments that they, or their family members, play.

"He'll laugh," said my sister.

14

I decided not to take my teddy bear.

15

That afternoon, I played with Reggie.
Reggie had plans, big plans.
"Tonight," he said, "when you come to my house, we are going to have fun, fun, fun. First, I'll show you my junk collection. And after that we'll have a wrestling match. And after that, a pillow fight. And after that we'll do magic tricks. And after that we'll play checkers. And after that we'll play dominoes. And after that we can fool around with my magnifying glass."
"Great!" I said. "I can hardly wait."

"By the way," I asked, "what do you think of teddy bears?"

17

Students Acquiring English

Idioms Note the phrase *by the way*. If children are confused, explain that people use this expression when they are talking together and one person wants to start talking about something new. Here, Ira wanted to ask Reggie about teddy bears.

Science Link

Display a magnifying glass and ask if children know what it can do. Invite them to see how a magnifying glass makes objects larger. Have children tell how such a tool might make learning about small items, such as bugs, easier.

READ ALOUD

But Reggie just went on talking and planning as if he had never heard of teddy bears. "And after that," he said, "do you know what we can do after that—I mean when the lights are out and the house is really dark? Guess what we can do?"
"What?" I asked.
"We can tell ghost stories."
"Ghost stories?" I said.
"Ghost stories," said Reggie, "scary, creepy, spooky ghost stories."
I began to think about my teddy bear.

"Does your house get very dark?" I asked.
"Uh-huh," said Reggie.
"Very, very dark?"
"Uh-huh," said Reggie.
"By the way," I said again, "what do you think of teddy bears?"

Suddenly, Reggie was in a big hurry to go someplace.
"See you tonight," he said.
"See you," I said.

I decided to take my teddy bear.

"Good," said my mother.
"Good," said my father.

But my sister said:

23

"What if Reggie wants to know your teddy
bear's name. Did you think about that?
And did you think about how he will laugh
and say Tah Tah is a silly, baby name,
even for a teddy bear?"
"He won't ask," I said.
"He'll ask," she said.

I decided not to take my teddy bear.

25

Visual Literacy

Point out the street sign on page 19,
noting that many street signs use
pictures instead of words. Invite
children to think of other street
signs that use pictures. They might
like to draw some of the signs they
have seen.

Interact *with* Literature

READ ALOUD

At last, it was time to go to Reggie's house.
"Good night," said my mother.
"Good night," said my father.
"Sleep tight," said my sister.

26

I went next door where Reggie lived.

27

Reading Strategies

▶ Summarize

Teacher Modeling Tell children that thinking about the important parts of a story can help them to understand and remember it. Help children retell what has happened up to the time Ira leaves for Reggie's house by displaying the illustrations as you model retelling the story.

Think Aloud

The first thing that happens is that Ira says he is going to sleep over at Reggie's house. Then Ira can't decide if he should take his teddy bear with him. First he decides not to take the bear because his sister says Reggie will laugh. When Reggie talks about ghost stories, though, he decides to take the bear. But when his sister says Tah Tah is a silly baby name, Ira changes his mind again and decides not to take his bear.

Have children now use the illustrations to retell the story patterning their retelling after the model above.

That night, Reggie showed me his junk. He showed me his flashlight, his collection of bottle caps, a chain made of chewing gum wrappers, some picture postcards, an egg timer, jumbo goggles, a false nose and mustache, and a bunch of old rubber stamps and labels from his father's office.

We decided to play "office" with the rubber stamps.

28

QuickREFERENCE

Social Studies Link

Talk about where Reggie lives, noting that Ira just hops over a railing to get to his house. Explain that Ira and Reggie live in attached houses, sometimes called town houses, condos, or row houses. Invite children to name different kinds of homes.

Students Acquiring English
MEETING INDIVIDUAL NEEDS

Idioms Contrast the different ways of saying the phrase *sleep tight* (page 26). Ask children to say *sleep tight* in a nice way and then the way Ira's sister might say it.

Visual Literacy

Have children identify the flashlight, bottle caps, gum wrapper chain, postcards, egg timer, goggles, false nose and mustache on page 28 by pointing to them in the picture.

After that we had a
wrestling match.

And after that we had
a pillow fight.

30

And after that Reggie's father said:

31

"Bedtime!"

32

"Already?" said Reggie.
"Already," said his father.
We got into bed.
"Good night," said Reggie's father.
"Good night," we said.

33

Read Aloud pp. 30–33

Visual Literacy

Point out the rubber stamp imprints and the labels on page 29. Ask where children have seen labels like these. (on letters, packages; in their parents' offices) Display rubber stamps and labels for children to examine.

MEETING INDIVIDUAL NEEDS

Challenge

Encourage children to tell what the sign on the wall (page 33) says. (stop) Ask them where they usually see such a sign. Invite them to tell a word that means the opposite. (go)

★★★ Multicultural Link

Invite children who know how to say *good night* in other languages to teach the words to the class, for example: Portuguese—*boa noite*; Japanese—*oya-sumi nassaai*; Russian—*spakoyni nochi*.

Phonemic Awareness

Produces Alliteratives

TESTED SKILL

Teach/Model

Remind children that some words begin with the same sound. Ask children to listen as you name two things in Reggie's room: *false nose, picture postcards.* Ask which words begin with the same sound. (*picture postcards*) Model how children can also think of other words that begin with the sound in *picture postcards*.

Think Aloud

When I listen carefully to the words *picture* and *postcards*, I know they begin with the same sound – the sound for *p*. Since I know the beginning sound, I can think of other words I know that have this beginning sound, like *puppy* and *puzzle*.

Practice/Apply

Have children draw a picture of and say the name of another word that begins with the same sound they hear in each pair following: Reggie's room, haunted house, Foo Foo and Tah Tah.

Reread the pairs of words, inviting children to share their responses.

SKILL FINDER Name the Animals, page T127

Interact *with* Literature

Reading Strategies

▶ **Evaluate**

Teacher Modeling Help children evaluate Reggie's actions on pages 34 through 39. To help them, ask:

- What made Reggie suddenly go get his teddy bear while he was telling a ghost story?

- Why does Reggie make Ira promise not to laugh before he tells what his teddy bear's name is?

Then have children think about how Reggie becomes scared and gets his own teddy bear and how this is similar to Ira's wanting his own teddy bear. Ask how the two friends might have solved their teddy bear problem earlier in the day.

READ ALOUD

Reggie sighed.
I sighed.
"We can still tell ghost stories," said Reggie.
"Do you know any?" I asked.
"Uh-huh," said Reggie.

34

Reggie began to tell a ghost story:

"Once there was this ghost and he lived in a haunted house only he did most of the haunting himself. This house was empty except for this ghost because nobody wanted to go near this house, they were so afraid of this ghost. And every night this ghost would walk around this house and make all kinds of clunky, creeky sounds. *Aroomp! Aroomp!* Like that. And he would go around looking for people to scare because that's what he liked most to do: scare people. And he was very scary to look at. Oh, was he scary to look at!"

35

Reggie stopped.
"Are you scared?" he asked.
"Uh-huh," I said. "Are you?"
"What?" said Reggie.
"Are you scared?"
"Just a minute," said Reggie,
"I have to get something."

36

"What do you have to get?" I asked.
"Oh, something," said Reggie.
Reggie pulled the something out of a drawer.
The room was dark, but I could see it had fuzzy arms and legs and was about the size of a teddy bear.
I looked again. It was a teddy bear.

37

QuickREFERENCE

Vocabulary

Onomatopoeia Note the word *Aroomp* on page 35 that Reggie uses to name the sound the ghost makes. Invite children to suggest other ghostly sound words. (*boo, creak, clang, whooo*)

Reggie got back into bed.
"Now, about this ghost . . ." he said.
"Is that your teddy bear?" I asked.
"What?" said Reggie.
"Is that your teddy bear?"
"You mean this teddy bear?"
"The one you're holding," I said.
"Uh-huh," Reggie answered.
"Do you sleep with him all of the time?"
"What?" said Reggie.
"Do you sleep with him all of the time?"
"Uh-huh."
"Does your teddy bear have a name? Does
your teddy bear have a name?" I said louder.
"Uh-huh," Reggie answered.
"What is it?"
"You won't laugh?" said Reggie.
"No, I won't laugh," I said.
"Promise?"
"I promise."
"It's Foo Foo."
"Did you say 'Foo Foo'?"
"Uh-huh," said Reggie.

"Just a minute," I said, "I have
to get something."
"What do you have to get?" Reggie asked.
"Oh, something," I answered.

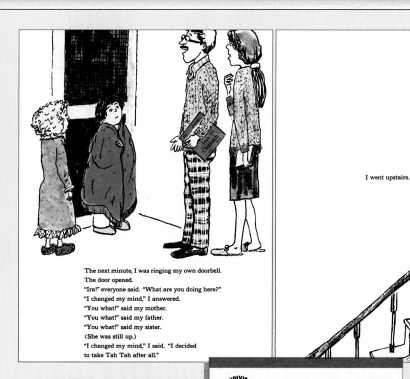

The next minute, I was ringing my own doorbell.
The door opened.
"Ira!" everyone said. "What are you doing here?"
"I changed my mind," I answered.
"You what!" said my mother.
"You what!" said my father.
"You what!" said my sister.
(She was still up.)
"I changed my mind," I said. "I decided
to take Tah Tah after all."

I went upstairs.

Challenge

Invite children to tell what two words
they hear in each of the following
words: *doorbell* (door, bell), *upstairs*
(up, stairs), *something* (some, thing).

🏠 Home Connection

Encourage children to find out
what kinds of reading materials
their parents enjoy. Invite them to
share their findings with the class.

2

Interact *with* Literature

READ ALOUD

Soon, I was down again
with Tah Tah.

My sister said:

43

Reading Strategies

▶ **Summarize**

Teacher Modeling Explain that one way children can be sure they remember a story is by retelling it in their own words. As children retell the story, remind them to think about Ira's problem and all the times he changes his mind. Display the following pages to help them retell the story:

- pages 10-11: Ira's problem

- pages 14-15: why Ira decides not to take his teddy bear

- pages 20-21: why Ira changes his mind and decides to take his teddy bear

- pages 24-25: why Ira decides not to take Tah Tah

- pages 38-39: why Ira goes home to get Tah Tah

"Reggie will laugh.
You'll see how he'll laugh.
He's just going to fall
down laughing."

"He won't laugh," said my mother.
"He won't laugh," said my father.

44

"He won't laugh," I said.

45

Self-Assessment

Remind children that good readers look for important things to remember. Ask children to tell how thinking about the important parts of the story helps them to remember and retell it.

QuickREFERENCE

Extra Support

Idioms If children seem confused by the phrases *fall down laughing* on page 44 and *fallen asleep* on page 47, discuss their meaning. Invite children to pantomime "falling down laughing" and "falling asleep."

I came back to Reggie's room.
"I have a teddy bear, too," I said. "Do you
want to know his name?"
I waited for Reggie to say, Uh-huh.
But Reggie didn't say, Uh-huh.
Reggie didn't say anything.

I looked at Reggie.
He was fast asleep. Just like that,
he had fallen asleep.
"Reggie! Wake up!" I said. "You have
to finish telling the ghost story."
But Reggie just held his teddy bear
closer and went right on sleeping.

And after that —
well, there wasn't anything to do
after that.
"Good night," I whispered to Tah Tah.
And I fell asleep, too.

48

Interact with Literature

Rereading

Choices for Rereading

Changing His Mind

Extra Support How many times did Ira change his mind about taking his teddy bear? As you read, have children raise teddy bears or teddy bear cutouts each time Ira decides to take Tah Tah and each time he decides to not take Tah Tah. Ask children to make a tally mark on a sheet of paper each time they raise their bears. Follow up by helping them count the results.

Dramatize the Story

Call on volunteers to take the roles of Ira, Ira's sister, his mother, his father, Reggie, and Reggie's father. Invite the group to act out the story as you reread it aloud. Provide simple props, such as teddy bears, to make the dramatization more complete.

Independent Storytime

Ira Sleeps Over is available as a book and read-along cassette package (Houghton Mifflin). Borrow the tape from your school or local library for children to use independently. Place the book and tape in the Reading and Listening Center, and invite children to listen to the story at their leisure.

Informal Assessment

Use Story Talk or Retelling *Ira Sleeps Over* to assess children's general understanding of the story.

Responding

Choices for Responding

Story Talk

Place children in groups of three or four to talk about the story. Children might discuss:

- why Ira and Reggie take teddy bears to bed

- favorite cuddly toys they sleep with

- why Ira's sister teases him (Is she teasing Ira to be mean? Or, is she just acting the way brothers and sisters sometimes act?)

- what might happen the next time Ira sleeps over (Will he take Tah Tah?)

Retelling *Ira Sleeps Over*

Have children work in small groups to retell the story using the teddy bear story props. Each group member should assume a character's role and respond accordingly as the story is retold.

> **Materials**
> - Story Retelling Props teddy bears (See Teacher's Handbook, page H4.)

What's in the Bag?

Note that Ira took an overnight bag to sleep over at Reggie's house. Have children think about what Ira packed in the bag. Ask them to draw or write their responses, then share them with the class. Tally the results for discussion.

Things to Pack	How Many Say This?
pajamas	~~HHH~~ ~~HHH~~ //
toothpaste	~~HHH~~ ////
toothbrush	~~HHH~~ /
slippers	~~HHH~~ ////

🏠 Home Connection

Have children draw a picture of their favorite part of the story. Encourage them to write or dictate a sentence telling about that part. Then have children share their pictures with their families as they retell the story. Family members might share their own experiences of sleeping over at someone else's house and how they felt.

Portfolio Opportunity

For a writing sample, save children's responses to What's in the Bag?

3
Instruct *and* Integrate

Comprehension

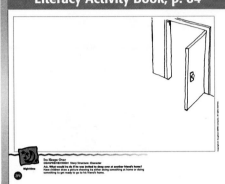

Practice Activities

Understanding Story Characters

LAB, p. 84

Extra Support Remind children that thinking about the things a story character says and does can help them learn more about that character. Review what children thought about the things Ira said and did. Then ask children to think about the other story characters.

- How does Ira's sister treat Ira? (teases, is hurtful) Would you want Ira's sister as a friend? Why or why not?

- What are Ira's parents like? (kind, understanding) Do you think Ira's parents are good parents?

- What kind of person is Reggie? (much like Ira; worried about what others will think and doesn't want his friends to think he's a baby)

- Do you think Reggie and Ira will have another sleep over?

Have children complete *Literacy Activity Book* page 84 to show what Ira might do if he were invited for another sleep over.

Characters in Other Stories

Choose a story children have previously read, such as *A Birthday Basket for Tia* and *Me Too!* or another class favorite. Reread the story, and pause now and then for children to comment on the actions of the characters. Prompt discussion by asking: Why did (character's name) do this? What does this tell us about (character's name)?

Story Characters and Me

Have children decide whether one of the story characters reminds them of themselves or someone they know. Have them draw the story character and the person they are reminded of. Suggest they write or dictate a sentence telling about their drawing.

Informal Assessment

As children complete the activities, note how well they understand the story characters. Also observe their ability to identify words with the same beginning sound.

Phonemic Awareness

Practice Activities

Name the Animals

LAB, p. 85

Ask children to say *Tah Tah*, listening for the beginning sounds. Then display a variety of stuffed animals. Invite groups of children to make up names for the animals that begin with the same sound. As groups share the names, list them on chart paper. Make name tags for the class favorites and tie them to the animals with string.

Then have children complete *Literacy Activity Book* page 85 to identify and suggest words that begin with the same sounds.

Recognizes Rhymes

Extra Support Sing "Twinkle, Twinkle Little Star" with children. Then tell them that you are going to say two words from the song. If the words rhyme, they should stand up. Say the following pairs of words: *star, are; twinkle, how; high, sky; star, moon.*

Matching Rhyming Picture Cards

Pairs of children can play a card game in which they try to match pictures that rhyme.

- Children shuffle and deal five cards each.

- A player asks, for example, "Do you have a card that rhymes with goat." If the player makes a match, the cards are set aside.

- The player with the most matches at the end of the game wins.

Materials
- Picture Cards: *goat, boat, cat, hat, car, jar, pear, bear, net, jet*

Portfolio Opportunity

Save *Literacy Activity Book* page 85 as a record of children's ability to identify words that begin with the same sounds.

3

Instruct *and* Integrate

Oral Language

Poster

BEDTIME

Brush your teeth.

Read a story.

Turn out the light.

Choices for Oral Language

Acting Out Feelings

Invite children to think about how Ira felt at different points in the story. For instance, he felt happy at the beginning of the story but then felt worried when his sister asked about his teddy bear. Write their ideas on a chart, similar to the following:

Feelings	
happy	scared
worried	sleepy

Ask for volunteers to pantomime the feelings on the chart for the rest of the class to guess. Encourage them to use both facial expressions and body movements.

All Kinds of Stories

MEETING INDIVIDUAL NEEDS

Challenge Reggie wanted to tell scary ghost stories, but there are many different kinds of stories. Have children make a list of the different kinds of stories they like to read.

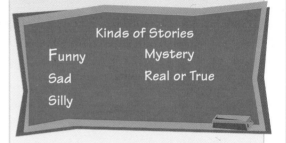

Kinds of Stories

Funny   Mystery

Sad   Real or True

Silly

Have children draw and write labels for the categories of books. Then let them sort the books in the Reading and Listening Center according to these categories.

Bedtime Rituals

Display the poster for "Bedtime." Have children comment on what the child in the poster is doing to get ready for bed. Have children share their own bedtime rituals and whether they do any of the same activities shown on the poster. They may enjoy drawing a picture showing something they do each night before going to bed and then sharing their picture with a partner.

What Would You Take?

Place an overnight bag on a table. Have children imagine they are going to sleep over at a friend's house: What would they take with them? List their ideas on index cards, and ask children to illustrate the cards with simple pictures. Place the cards in a pocket chart, and invite children to take turns packing the suitcase. Encourage them to tell why they chose each item.

Informal Assessment

- As children work on their oral language activities, note how well they are able to participate and respond.

- As they complete the activities on page T129, note whether they are able to put their ideas into writing.

 # Writing

Choices for Writing

Picture Postcards

Recall Reggie's postcard collection and elicit that people often send postcards to friends and family when they visit a new or exciting place. Display postcards for children to examine, and point out where a person can write a message and an address on the postcard.

Distribute large index cards, and invite children to make their own picture postcards. Have them paste or draw a picture of a place they would like to visit on one side of the card. On the other side, have them write or dictate a sentence to tell what they would do there.

Students Acquiring English Encourage children who are learning English to draw a picture that shows an interesting spot from the place where they were born. Let them take home their card and work with a family member to write a sentence in their native language.

Sharing My Special Things

Turn back to page 28 in *Ira Sleeps Over*. Read or use the illustrations to discuss Reggie's special collection of things — his "junk" that he shares with Ira at the sleep over. Have children draw a picture of the special things they would share with a friend at a sleep over. Encourage them to write or dictate labels for the things in their pictures and write a sentence telling about their special things.

A Surprise Twist

MEETING INDIVIDUAL NEEDS

Challenge Reread Reggie's ghost story on page 35, and point out that Reggie never finished his story because he became scared. Invite partners to discuss ways that Reggie's scary ghost story could turn into a silly or funny story about a ghost. Once children have made several different suggestions, have them draw a picture of their story idea and write or dictate sentences telling what happens. Encourage them to share their new versions with the class.

Portfolio Opportunity

Save children's responses to the activities on this page as writing samples.

Instruct *and* Integrate

Cross-Curricular Activities

Math

Sorting it Out

Ask children how Reggie might keep his junk collection in order. Invite them to show what they would do by scattering a few postcards, bottle caps, and rubber stamps on a table top for children to sort and put away in empty shoe boxes. Discuss why children sorted the items as they did.

Extra Support Extend the activity by having children work in small groups to classify classroom collections in a variety of ways. For example, children might sort building blocks by size, shape, or color.

Materials
- postcards
- bottle caps
- rubber stamps
- three empty shoe boxes
- classroom "collections" such as blocks, books, stuffed animals, toy cars and trucks, dolls, and so on.

Science

Under Glass

Provide children with hand-held magnifying glasses and a variety of items to examine. You might display a sea shell, a pebble, a leaf, a piece of bark, grains of sand, a fingerprint, a color photo from a magazine, and so on. Encourage children to compare what the object looks like without the magnifying glass and what it looks like under the glass.

Materials
- hand-held magnifying glasses
- a variety of small items such as: sea shell, pebble, leaf, piece of bark, sand, fingerprint, magazine photo

Social Studies

A Place to Call Home

Have children brainstorm a list of different kinds of homes. (row house, apartment, condominium, duplex, farmhouse, houseboat, trailer home) They might look through old magazines for pictures of different homes to include in a bulletin board display. Or, they can draw their own pictures of the homes in their community.

Materials
- old magazines
- scissors
- paste
- drawing paper
- markers or crayons

Art

Making an Impression

Ira and Reggie made their impressions with rubber stamps. Children, however, can have just as much fun making sponge prints.

1. Use markers to trace a moon or star shapes on a sponge.

2. Cut out the shape.

3. Dip the surface of the sponge into a thin layer of paint.

4. Press the painted side of the sponge onto a sheet of drawing paper to make prints.

Materials
- crescent moon and star stencils
- markers
- flat sponges
- scissors
- poster paints
- paper plates
- drawing paper

BIG BOOK
SELECTION:
Golden Bear

by Ruth Young
illustrated by
Rachel Isadora

Other Books by Ruth Young

Daisy's Taxi

The New Baby

A Trip to Mars

Big Book

Little Big Book

Selection Summary

In rhyming verse and bold illustrations, Ruth Young tells the story of the special relationship a young boy shares with his stuffed companion, Golden Bear. Together they learn to do many things, such as play the violin, talk to bugs, and make a snowman. Then at night, they wish on the first star and share a night filled with dreams.

Lesson Planning Guide

	Skill/Strategy Instruction	Meeting Individual Needs	Lesson Resources
1 **Introduce** *the* **Literature** *Pacing: 1 days*	**Shared Reading and Writing** Warm-up/Build Background, T134 Shared Reading, T134 Shared Writing, T135	Choices for Rereading, T135	**Poster** My Teddy Bear *Literacy Activity Book* Personal Response, p. 87
2 **Interact** *with* **Literature** *Pacing: 1-2 days*	**Reading Strategies** Predict/Infer, T136 Evaluate, T136, T138, T142, T148 Think About Words, T140, T144 Self-Question, T146 Monitor, T146 Summarize, T148 **Minilessons** ✓ High-Frequency Word: *have*, T137 ✓ Initial *b*, T139 ✓ Phonogram *-ug*, T141 ✓ Fantasy/Realism, T143 ✓ Directionality: Words, T145	Students Acquiring English, T149 Extra Support, T136, T139, T144, T150 Literature Link, T142 Rereading and Responding, T150–T151	**Letter, Word, and Picture Cards,** T137, T139 *Literacy Activity Book* Language Patterns, p. 88 **Audio Tape** for Nighttime: *Golden Bear* See the Houghton Mifflin **Internet** resources for additional activities
3 **Instruct** *and* **Integrate** *Pacing: 1-2 days*	**Reading/Listening Center,** Comprehension, T152 Phonics/Decoding, T153–T154 Concepts About Print, T155 Vocabulary, T156 Listening, T157 **Language/Writing Center,** Oral Language, T158 Writing, T159 **Cross-Curricular Center,** Cross-Curricular Activities, T160–T161	Challenge, T154, T158	**Poster** Twinkle Twinkle Little Star **Letter, Word, and Picture Cards,** T153, T154, T156, T158 **Story Props,** T151 **My Big Dictionary,** T153 *Literacy Activity Book* Comprehension, p. 89 Phonics/Decoding, pp. 91–92 Vocabulary, p. 93 **Audio Tape** for Nighttime: *Golden Bear* See the Houghton Mifflin **Internet** resources for additional activities

✓ *Indicates Tested Skills. See page T105 for assessment options.*

1

Introduce *the* Literature

Shared Reading and Writing

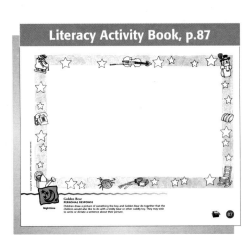

Poster

Poster

MY TEDDY BEAR

A teddy bear is nice to hold.
The one I have is getting old.
His paws are almost wearing out
And so's his funny furry snout
From rubbing on my nose of skin,
And all his fur is pretty thin.
A ribbon and a piece of string
Make a sort of necktie thing.
His eyes came out and now instead
He has some new ones made of thread.
I take him *everywhere* I go
And tell him all the things I know.
I like the way he feels at night,
All snuggled up against me tight.

MARGARET HILLERT

Literacy Activity Book, p.87

INTERACTIVE LEARNING

Warm-up/Build Background

Sharing Poetry
- Read aloud the "My Teddy Bear" poster.
- Ask how the child in the poem feels about the teddy bear. Why does the child like to bring the teddy bear everywhere?
- Read the poem again, pausing for children to supply the rhyming words. Focus attention on the last four lines of the poem. Invite children to suggest places the child might take the teddy bear. What things would the child tell the teddy bear?

Shared Reading

LAB, p. 87

Preview and Predict
- Display *Golden Bear*. Point to and read aloud the title and the names of the author and illustrator. Briefly discuss the cover, asking children to point out Golden Bear.
- Take a picture walk through page 17, inviting children to comment on the illustrations. Help them use picture details to predict what the selection will be about.
- Encourage children to predict what things the boy and Golden Bear might do together. List their predictions on chart paper for later use.

Read Together
- Read the story aloud, emphasizing the rhyming words. Encourage children to join in with the rhymes and with other words they may know.
- As you read, invite children to comment on the illustrations. Pause now and then for children to match their predictions against what happens in the story.
- Encourage children to check the predictions on the chart paper.

Personal Response
Have children complete *Literacy Activity Book* page 87 to show which thing the boy and Golden Bear did together that they also like to do.

Shared Writing: *A Class Poem*

Brainstorming

Recall some of the things the boy and Golden Bear did together. Then invite children to write additional verses to tell about the things the boy and Golden Bear might do together. Brainstorm a list of activities to write about.

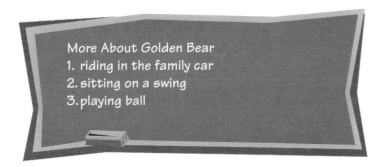

More About Golden Bear
1. riding in the family car
2. sitting on a swing
3. playing ball

Drafting

Have children contribute lines to the class poem. Record their suggestions on chart paper. Help children create a rhyming line to accompany each line they suggest.

Think Aloud

Our first line is *riding in the family car*. Let's think of words that rhyme with car, such as *star* and *jar*. (Pause for children to suggest other rhymes.) Can you think of something the boy and Golden Bear might do in the car that tells about one of these rhyming words? (making wishes on a star, catching fireflies in a jar)

Publishing

Copy the lines of the class poem onto drawing paper, and ask volunteers to illustrate them. Bind the pages into a class book for the Reading and Listening Center.

Choices for Rereading

Rereadings enable children to focus on different aspects of a story and to respond to it in varying ways. Use some or all of the rereading choices on page T150.

- Listen and Read
- Listening for Initial *b*
- Reading for Rhyme
- Exploring Language Patterns

Portfolio Opportunity

Save *Literacy Activity Book* page 87 as a record of children's personal response to the story.

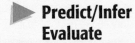

Interact *with* Literature

Dancing up the golden stair

Reading Strategies

▶ **Predict/Infer**
Evaluate

Discussion Remind children of the things good readers can do to help them understand and remember a story: they make predictions about a story; they think about what they hear and read.

Review the predictions children made before reading *Golden Bear*.

- Did they make good use of picture clues and their own backgrounds to make reasonable predictions?

- Were they surprised at any of the things the boy and Golden Bear did?

Guide children in asking questions about the things that surprised them. For example: Could a teddy bear really dance up the stairs?

Purpose Setting

As children reread the story with you, have them think about which things Golden Bear could really do with the boy and which things the boy only imagines the teddy bear doing.

QuickREFERENCE

High-Frequency Words Review

Remind children that they have learned to read the word *I*. Ask a volunteer to find this word on page 7. Have children identify the boy as "I," or the speaker in the story.

Extra Support

Referents Make sure children see that the word *him* on page 7 names Golden Bear and not the boy. If necessary, reread the sentence substituting the words *Golden Bear* for the word *him*.

Concept Development Review

Color Words Ask children to name the bear's color. (gold) Have children name other things that are gold.

Golden Bear, Golden Bear,
I have seen him everywhere:

7

High-Frequency Word: *have*

TESTED SKILL

Teach/Model

Display Magic Picture *horse*, recalling that it begins with the sound for *h*. Ask children to listen as you read the words on page 7 and name two words that begin with the sound for *h*. *(have, him)*

Display Word Card *have*. Read *have* aloud, emphasizing the initial consonant. Ask a child to find *have* on the page. If he or she points to the word *him*, compare the words letter for letter. Then invite children to help you read the page, pausing for them to supply the words *I* and *have*.

Practice/Apply

Display this sentence:

"I have the ⬤ ."

Also display Picture Cards: *ball, balloon, bike, book.* First have children read the sentence; then remove the picture and have children add new Picture Cards in the blank. Have children read their new sentences.

SKILL FINDER What Do You Have Golden Bear?, page T156

Phonemic Awareness Review

Rhyming Words Have children listen for rhyming words as you read page 7. *(bear, everywhere)* Have them listen for a word that rhymes with *bear* and *everywhere* on page 8. *(stair)*

Phonics/Decoding Review

Have children listen as you read page 8. Ask what sound they hear at the beginning of the word *dancing*. *(d)* Encourage children to suggest other words that begin with the sound for *d*.

Interact *with* Literature

Rocking in my rocking chair

10

Reading Strategies

▶ **Evaluate**

Discussion Remind children that good listeners and readers decide what they think about a story. Encourage children to share their ideas about what the boy and the bear are doing on pages 10 and 11. Is reading a book and rocking in a rocking chair a good activity to do with a stuffed bear? Would they enjoy doing this with a stuffed animal?

Follow a similar procedure to encourage children to evaluate the text and pictures on pages 12 and 13.

QuickREFERENCE

 Journal

After children read the story, suggest they draw or write about some things the boy does with Golden Bear that they also like to do with their cuddly toys.

 Students Acquiring English

Use the pictures on pages 6–14 to help children understand the meaning of *golden, stair, rocking chair, violin,* and *chin.*

11

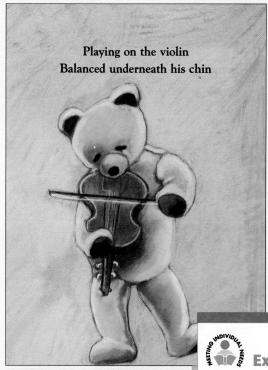

Playing on the violin
Balanced underneath his chin

Big Book pp. 11, 13

MINILESSON

Phonics/Decoding
Initial *b*

Teach/Model

Display the cover of the Big Book. Call on a volunteer to read the title aloud, pointing to the words as they are read. Have a child frame the word *Bear* and name the first letter in the word. *(b)* Ask children to say *bear*, listening for the beginning sound.

Recall with children that Magic Pictures help them remember the sounds for letters. Display Magic Picture *bird* and have it identified.

Have children say *bear* and *bird*, listening for the beginning sounds.

Practice/Apply

Read page 13, asking children to listen for a word that begins with the /b/ sound. *(balanced)* Have them say *bird, bear,* and *balanced*, listening for the beginning sounds. Then frame *balanced* and have the initial letter identified. *(b)*

SKILL FINDER Reading *B* Words, page T153

Extra Support

Word Meaning Most children will know the word *balanced* as it applies to walking on a beam or riding a bike. Show how a violin is balanced by balancing a violin or a long object, such as a baseball bat, under your chin.

Music Link

Invite children to tell what they know about violins. Note that a violin makes music when the bow is pulled across the strings or when the strings are plucked.

Interact *with* Literature

Reading Strategies

▶ Think About Words

Discuss how children could figure out the word *bug* on page 14. The line says:

Cozy on the big green rug
Talking to a little_____

- **What makes sense** This word names something little on the rug. From the pattern of the story, I know the word must rhyme with *rug.*

- **Sounds for letters** What letter does the word begin with? *(b)* What word rhymes with *rug,* begins with the sound for *b,* and names something little?

- **Picture clues** The picture shows the boy and Golden Bear talking to a bug. I think the word is *bug.*

Have children reread the lines on page 14 with you. Ask if the word *bug* makes sense.

Cozy on the big green rug
Talking to a little bug

14

Skating fast on silver ice
Tracing perfect circles twice

16

QuickREFERENCE

Vocabulary

Word Meaning Note that the word *cozy* means "comfortable." The boy and the bear are comfortable as they sit on the rug watching the bug. Encourage children to name other cozy places the boy and Golden Bear might enjoy.

Science Link

Ask if children can name the little bug. If necessary, tell children that it is a ladybug. These small beetles help people by eating other bugs (aphids) that harm plants.

Phonics/Decoding

Phonogram -ug

TESTED SKILL

Teach/Model

Reread the lines on page 14, asking children to listen for the rhyming words. Then write *rug* and *bug*, one under the other, on the board.

Ask children to compare the words. (They begin with different consonants; end with the letters *-ug*.) Then display the following letters along the chalkboard ledge and model using them:

d   m   h

Think Aloud I can use what I know about the sounds for letters to make new words that end with *-ug*. (Write *dug* on the board.) This word has the same ending sounds as *rug* and *bug* and begins with the sound for *d*. The word is *dug*.

Practice/Apply

Invite children to help you create new words for *m* and *h*. Have them read the words *mug* and *hug*.

Ask children to draw pictures for two of the words. Have them label their drawings.

SKILL FINDER   Spelling Words with *-ug*, page T154

Math Link

Mention that the word *twice* means "two times." Ask children to use picture clues to tell what number the boy and Golden Bear make. Write the number 8 on the board to show the link between the two circles and the numeral 8.

MEETING INDIVIDUAL NEEDS   Challenge

Encourage children to tell what happens to a pond in an area where there are four very different seasons. (winter–freezes; spring–melts; summer–gets warmer; fall–gets colder.)

Science Link

Have children use picture clues to tell what time of year is shown on pages 16-17. (winter) Mention that in many parts of the country, water freezes and turns to ice in the winter. Ask what the boy might see when the ice melts. (pond, lake)

Interact *with* Literature

Making snowmen in the snow

18

Watching tulips start to grow

20

Reading Strategies

▶ **Evaluate**

Discussion Point out that picture clues can also help readers think about a story. Have children look at the picture of Golden Bear on pages 18-19 and on pages 20-21. Ask children if stuffed teddy bears are usually the same size as their owners. Encourage children to use the picture clues to tell what the artist may want readers to think of Golden Bear. (Examples: the artist made Golden Bear "life-size" so readers will see how important it is to the boy; to help readers think of it as real; to see the bear the size the boy imagines it to be)

Quick**REFERENCE**

Literature Link

Children may enjoy reviewing how snowmen are made by rereading the Watch Me Read book, *Snow Fun*.

Comprehension

Fantasy/ Realism

TESTED SKILL

Teach/Model

Tell children that in this story some of the things the boy and Golden Bear do together are things that a boy could do with a stuffed animal in real life. Other things are make-believe — they couldn't happen in real life. Reread pages 18-21, and model for children how to think about which activities could and which could not happen in real life.

Think Aloud

In the beginning of the story when Golden Bear and the boy were sitting and reading a book, I thought about how I like to do that with my stuffed animals. I know that a stuffed teddy bear could also sit beside me to watch flowers grow. But a teddy bear couldn't really help me build a snowman. That is make-believe.

Practice/Apply

Invite children to review other pages in the story to name those things a child could do with a teddy bear and those things that a child could only imagine a teddy bear doing.

SKILL FINDER

Fantasy and Realism in *Golden Bear*, page T152

Minilessons, Themes 4 and 10

Science Link

Help children use text and picture clues to conclude that a tulip is a kind of flower. Invite children to name other flowers they know.

Interact
with
Literature

In the garden planting seeds
Making mudpies, pulling weeds

22

Reading Strategies

▶ **Think About Words**

Discuss how children could figure out the word *seeds* on page 22.

The line says: *In the garden planting* _____

- **What makes sense** This word names something you plant in a garden. From the pattern of the story, I know the word must rhyme with *weeds*.

- **Sounds for letters** What letter does the word begin with? *(s)* What word rhymes with *weeds*, begins with the sound for *s*, and is something you plant in a garden? *(seeds)*

Have children reread the lines on page 22 with you. Ask if the word *seeds* makes sense.

QuickREFERENCE

Extra Support

Explain that children make mudpies when they are "pretend baking." The mud "batter" is made out of water and dirt and shaped into pies. Invite children who have made mudpies to share their experiences.

Science Link

Have children use text and picture clues to tell what time of year is shown on pages 22-23. (spring) Have them name the clues. (text: planting seeds, pulling weeds; picture: how the boy is dressed, the flowers growing)

Talking on the telephone
With me when I'm all alone

25

Concepts About Print

Directionality: Words

Teach/Model

Display pages 22-23. Remind children that words on a page are read in a certain way — from the left side to the right side of the page. Call on a volunteer to point to the first word to be read on this page. Read the word *In* aloud. Then have the child point to the next word to be read, and read the word *the*.

Now tell children that the letters in each word are also read in a certain way — from the left side to the right side of the word. Display the word *seed* on the board. Point to and model reading the word from left to right.

Think Aloud

The word *seed* begins with the letter *s*. When I read the word *seed*, the first letter I look at is *s*. The next letter is *e*, another *e*, and finally *d*. When I write the word *seed* first I write *s*, then *e*, then another *e*, and then *d*.

Practice/Apply

Repeat the procedure with other words from the story. Frame individual words on the page, asking children to name the letters in the words from left to right.

SKILL FINDER | Directionality: Words, page 155

Interact *with* Literature

26

Reading Strategies

▶ **Self-Question/ Monitor**

Discussion Remind children that good readers ask themselves questions to make sure they understand what is happening in a story. As you reread pages 26-29, encourage children to think about questions such as:

- Could a teddy bear keep a boy company at bathtime?

- Would I do the things the boy and Golden Bear do with one of my stuffed animals?

Quick**REFERENCE**

Literature Link

Invite children to share stories they may know about pirates, such as *Peter Pan* or *Treasure Island*. Note that *Yo, ho, ho*, are words that pirates like to say.

Health Link

Ask if children have ever seen the symbol on the pirate ship flag on page 26. Explain that things labeled with this sign contain something dangerous or harmful. Children should never eat, drink, or touch something with this label.

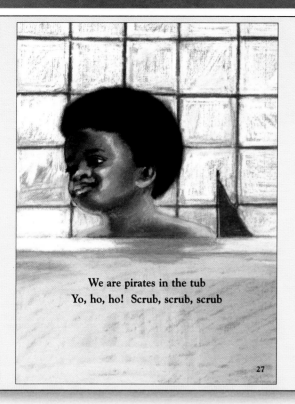

We are pirates in the tub
Yo, ho, ho! Scrub, scrub, scrub

27

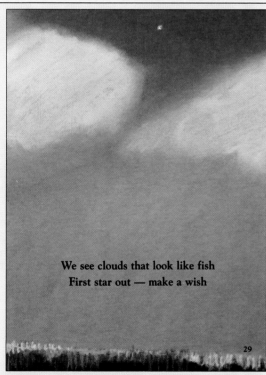

We see clouds that look like fish
First star out — make a wish

29

Interact *with* Literature

Dreaming dreamy dreams at night
Golden Bear tucked in tight.

30

Reading Strategies

▶ **Evaluate**

Discussion Invite children to share their feelings about the story:

• Did you like this story?

• What parts of the story seemed make-believe? What parts seemed real?

• Did anything in the story remind you of things you have done?

▶ **Summarize**

Discussion Talk about how good readers and listeners think about the most important parts of a story to help them remember it.

To help children, tell them to imagine that they are retelling the story to a friend who wants to read it. Have children role-play summarizing the story to a partner. Point out that they don't need to tell everything that happens, just the important parts.

Self-Assessment

Encourage children to think about their reading by asking these questions:

• Were you confused about anything you were reading?

• What did you do if you didn't understand something?

31

QuickREFERENCE

Students
Acquiring English

MEETING INDIVIDUAL NEEDS

Use the picture to help children understand that the phrase *tucked in tight* means "snugly placed under the bed covers." Ask children who tucks them in at night. You might also want to remind children of the phrase *sleep tight* in *Ira Sleeps Over*.

2

Interact *with* Literature

Rereading

Golden Bear, Golden Bear,
I have seen him

Choices for Rereading

Listen and Read

Audio Tape for Nighttime:
Golden Bear

Children can be independent readers by following along in the Little Big Book as they play the Audio Tape. Invite them to read along in their books as they listen to the tape.

Students Acquiring English The Audio Tape provides support for children who are learning English. It allows them to listen to the words as they look at the pictures, thus reinforcing their language learning.

Listening for Initial *b*

Extra Support As you read the story, have children listen for beginning sounds. Ask them to clap each time they hear a word that begins with the sound for *b*. Pause a few times to frame the *b* word; have the initial letter identified. You could repeat this activity for other initial consonants they have learned: *m, s, h, d.*

Real Teddy Bear

As you reread the story, have children hold up a cutout of a teddy bear each time a picture shows something that a child could really do with a teddy bear.

Exploring Language Patterns

LAB, p. 88

To focus on the rhyming words, reread *Golden Bear* slowly, pointing to the words. After reading a line of text, invite children to supply the rhyming word that ends the next line.

Provide practice with story language patterns by having children complete *Literacy Activity Book* page 88.

Informal Assessment

Use the Story Talk or the retelling activity to assess children's general understanding of the selection.

Responding

Choices for Responding

Personal Response

Invite children to work with a partner to pantomime and narrate their favorite scene from the story. One child can act out the scene while the other narrates. They might also pantomime scenes without narration and invite the class to guess which scene they are doing. Children can then discuss which parts of the story seemed to be the favorites based on the activity.

Story Talk

Place children in groups of two or three, and have them respond to one or more of the following:

- Do you have a cuddly toy like Golden Bear? What is it like?

- What things do the boy and Golden Bear do that you also like to do with your cuddly toy? What make-believe things do you do with your cuddly toy?

- Do you sleep with your cuddly toy? Why is it nice to have a cuddly toy at nighttime?

Retelling
Golden Bear

Have children work with partners to retell the story *Golden Bear* using a teddy bear. Encourage them to dramatize the activities that the boy and Golden Bear do in the story.

Materials
- Story Retelling Prop teddy bear (See Teacher's Handbook, page H4.)

 ### Home Connection

Have children trace and cut out bear shapes, decorate them to look like Golden Bear, and paste them onto sheets of paper. Then they can draw and label some of the things Golden Bear could do. Have them take their Golden Bear home to share with their families. They might also ask family members to share stories about cuddly toys they treasured as children.

Students Acquiring English Ask children to discuss with a family member pet animals or other dolls in their culture and report back to the class.

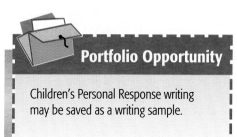
Portfolio Opportunity

Children's Personal Response writing may be saved as a writing sample.

Instruct *and* **Integrate**

Comprehension

Practice Activities

Fantasy and Realism in *Golden Bear*

LAB, p. 89

Extra Support Display *Golden Bear*, asking children to briefly recall what the story is about. Then take a picture walk through the story and invite children to discuss each spread in turn. Ask which pictures show things a teddy bear could do with the boy and which pictures show things the boy could only imagine the teddy bear doing.

Then have children complete *Literacy Activity Book* page 89 to show how well they can identify real and fanciful story elements.

What an Imagination!

Challenge Tell children that in *Golden Bear*, the boy uses his imagination to turn his teddy bear into a make-believe friend. Invite children to work with partners and use their imaginations to:

- Name pages that show things the teddy bear might do, such as sit in a rocking chair, and tell how to make the page make-believe. (Golden Bear reads to the boy.)

- Name pages that show make-believe things, such as the teddy bear ice skating, and tell how to make the page real. (Boy may skate with Golden Bear in his arms.)

Real and Make-Believe Game

- Make picture cards of animal characters doing real and make-believe things. (Use magazine pictures, newspaper cartoons, stencils, or hand drawn pictures.)

- On the back of the square, write "R" if the picture shows something that could happen in real life. Write "M" if it shows something that could only be make-believe.

- Have children work with a partner, guessing whether the picture is real or make-believe and then self checking their answers.

Informal Assessment

As children complete the activities, note how well they are able to distinguish between real and make-believe events. Also observe their skill in identifying initial /b/b words.

Phonics/Decoding

Practice Activities

Literacy Activity Book, p. 91

Reading *B* Words

LAB, p. 91

Extra Support Construct this sentence in a pocket chart:

"I have my boat," said the [ ].

Display Picture Cards *boat* and *jet*. Point to the word *boat* in the sentence, saying that this word names one of the pictures. Children can use what they know about the sound for *b* to read this word. Call on volunteers to read the sentence.

Repeat the procedure with the Picture Cards *bear* and *dog* and this sentence: "I have my bear," said the [boy.]

Home Connection Have children complete *Literacy Activity Book* page 91 to practice identifying other words that begin with the sound for *b*. Encourage children to take it home and point out all the *b* words on the page to a family member.

Materials
- Word Cards: *I, have, my, said, the*
- Index Cards: for making word cards for *bear* and *boat*
- Picture Cards: *bear, boat, boy, dog, jet*

Animals at Night

Give small groups of children tokens to play the game for additional practice on initial /b/*b* and other initial consonants.

Materials
- Game: Animals at Night (See Teacher's Handbook, page H8.)

My Big Dictionary

Display pages 6-7 of *My Big Dictionary*. Read the words on page 6 aloud to children, pointing to the initial *b* and emphasizing the sound /b/ as you read. Then invite partners to work together to find five things on page 7 that begin with the sound for *b*. You may want to encourage children to use temporary spellings and make a list of their words for their Journals.

My Big Dictionary

Portfolio Opportunity

- Record children's understanding of realism/fantasy by saving *Literacy Activity Book* page 89.
- Save children's work on My Big Dictionary for a record of their understanding of /b/ words.

Phonics/Decoding

I have a
bug mug.

The bug dug.

Golden Bear
PHONICS/DECODING Phonogram: -ug
Read the sentences with children and have them trace the letters to complete
each word. Then have them read the completed sentences and draw pictures to
illustrate them.

Practice Activities

Spelling Words with -*ug*

Extra Support Display Picture Card *rug*, and have children name it. Show children how to use the Phonogram Card -*ug* and Letter Card *r* to make the word *rug*. Read the word with children.

Display Letter Cards *d, h, m,* and *b* and Phonogram Card -*ug*. Then read aloud the following words and sentences. Have children write each word:

- *mug:* I drink milk from a *mug*.
- *bug:* A beetle is a kind of *bug*.
- *hug:* I like to give my bear a *hug*.
- *dug:* I *dug* a hole in the dirt.

Materials
- Letter Cards: *d, h, m, b, r*
- Picture Card: *rug*
- Phonogram Card: -*ug*

Reading -*ug* Words

Challenge Supply children with Letter Cards for *j* and *t* and have them make new words using these letters and the phonogram -*ug*. Have children read the words they made. Ask them which word completes each sentence:

- The milk is in the *jug*.
- He gave a *tug* on the rope.

Bugs, Bugs, Bugs

LAB, p. 92

Have children complete *Literacy Activity Book* page 92 to practice reading words with the phonogram -*ug*.

Students Acquiring English You might want to pair up children who are learning English with native speakers to work on their activity pages together.

Informal Assessment

As children complete the activities, note the ease with which they are able to recognize and read words with the phonogram -*ug*. Also observe their understanding of how words are read from left to right on a page.

Concepts About Print

Practice Activities

Directionality: Words

MEETING INDIVIDUAL NEEDS

Extra Support Recall that the words should be read in a certain order. Display "My Teddy Bear" poster, and ask children to help you read the poem aloud. Have a child point to the first word in the first line of the poem; read the word aloud. Then have the child point to the next word; read it aloud. Repeat the procedure across the line of text.

Help children apply left to right directionality to reading words. Frame the word *bear*. Have a child point to and name each letter in the word, from left to right. Ask what sound this word begins with. (the sound for *b*) Repeat the procedure with other words in the poem, such as *hold*, *make*, and *some*.

From Left to Right

Audio Tape for Nighttime: *Golden Bear*

Place copies of the Little Big Book along with the audio tape for partner reading. Tell them to use their finger to follow along with the words as the narrator reads the story. While children may not be able to follow the text word for word, they should be applying left to right directionality in their independent reading.

Word Boundaries: First Letter

Have children recall that each word begins with a certain letter. Open *Golden Bear* to page 16 and have children read the page with you. Point to and say the word *Skating*. Invite an interested child to point to the first letter in the word *Skating* and tell what letter this word begins with.

Play a guessing game in which you tell children you are thinking of another word on the page that begins with a certain letter. Volunteers should point to the word on the page that begins with the letter you name and read the word with you.

Vocabulary

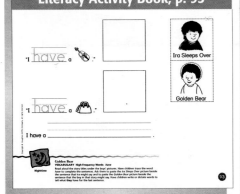

Literacy Activity Book, p. 93

Practice Activities

What Do You Have, Golden Bear?

LAB, p. 93

MEETING INDIVIDUAL NEEDS

Extra Support Assign a group of three children the roles of Boy, Golden Bear, and Guesser.

- The Boy uses Word and Picture Cards to construct a sentence for Golden Bear to read, for example: *I have the [banana]*.

- Golden Bear reads the sentence silently.

- The Guesser then asks, "What do you have, Golden Bear?"

- Golden Bear responds by reading the sentence aloud.

- Players switch roles to play again.

Give children additional practice reading the high-frequency words by having them complete *Literacy Activity Book* page 93.

Materials
- Word Cards: *I*, *the*, *have*
- Picture Cards for *b – banana, basket, bike, ball*

Bear Hunt

Cut out bear shapes and print each high-frequency word several times on the shapes. (Words: *have, I, my, said, the*) Hide the shapes around the room and have children go on a bear hunt. Have them collect all of the hidden bear shapes. Then children can read the words they found to you.

Have You Seen Golden Bear?

- Make several sets of index cards with high-frequency words written on them. Only one index card should read "I have!"

- Place the cards face down on a table. Tell children to search for the card that answers: *Have you seen Golden Bear?* Have children take turns choosing and reading a card.

- The child who uncovers the *I have!* card, reshuffles the cards and asks the question for another round of play.

Informal Assessment

As children complete the activities, note how easily they are able to recognize and read the high-frequency words. Also observe their skill at listening to information transmitted over a "phone."

Listening

Listening Activities

Bedtime Rhymes

Display the following bedtime rhymes and read them aloud. Invite children to share any other bedtime rhymes they know. You may wish to write some of their suggestions on chart paper. Then invite them to choose their favorite bedtime rhyme and illustrate it. Children may wish to copy the appropriate verse on their drawings and share them with their families.

Good night,	Good night,	Good night,
Sleep tight.	Sleep long.	Sleep tight.
Don't let	You'll grow up	Wake up bright,
The bed bugs bite.	Big and Strong.	In the morning light.

Students Acquiring English Encourage children to share rhymes or special "good nights" that they say in their native language.

Telephone Talk

One activity the boy and Golden Bear shared was talking on the telephone. Help children make telephones using string and empty cans. Have them use the telephones to role-play a conversation between the boy and Golden Bear. Have partners include the following telephone skills in their role-play:

- placing a telephone call and identifying themselves

- answering the telephone call

- ending the telephone call and saying good-bye

Students Acquiring English Children could practice this activity in their own language at home with a family member and then try it at school in English with a child who speaks fluent English.

Portfolio Opportunity

For a record of children's ability to write the high-frequency word *have,* save *Literacy Activity Book* page 93.

Instruct
and
Integrate

Oral Language

Choices for Oral Language

Materials
- Picture Cards: *fox, dog, cat, mouse*

Rhyming Language Patterns

Remind children that the story *Golden Bear* is written in rhyme. Display pages 14-15 and read the lines with children. Then write the following on sentence strips and display the picture cards:

| Cozy underneath a box | Talking to a little _____. |

Tell children that they can make a rhyme that names other places the boy and Golden Bear might find cozy. Read the lines with children. Have them suggest a word that rhymes with *box* and names one of the animals in the Picture Cards to complete the second line. Write *fox* on the second line, and have children read the new phrase.

Have children make additional verses. Then invite them to choose a favorite rhyme to copy and illustrate.

Names for Musical Instruments

Challenge Display page 12. Have children discuss the violin in the picture, noting that this instrument has strings. Have children name and categorize other instruments they know. For example, instruments that have strings (guitar, banjo); instruments that you blow into (flute, trumpet); instruments you play with your hands (percussion instruments: drums, xylophone, piano). Children might enjoy drawing pictures and labeling their favorite instruments.

Star Light, Star Bright

Ask if any children know the rhyme people say when they make a wish on a star. Display the rhyme and read it aloud with children.

Star light, star bright.
First star I see tonight.
I wish I may,
I wish I might,
Have the wish I wish tonight.

Have children repeat the rhyme several times until they know it. Then call on volunteers to recite the rhyme and make a wish.

Informal Assessment

As children work on making rhymes, note their ability to put together a rhyming pattern. Also observe whether they make an effort to figure out initial consonants of unknown words.

Writing

Choices for Writing

Star Wishes

Show children how to trace the stencil to make stars.

On one side of the star, have children write their names. On the other side, have them write, or dictate, a wish that they might make on the star. Invite children to place their stars, wish side up, on the Nighttime bulletin board.

Home Connection Extend the activity by inviting children to make star wishes for their families.

Materials
- sheets of unlined writing paper
- star stencils
- scissors

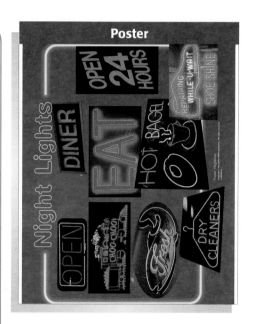

Poster

Under the Night Sky

Ask children to think of the things they enjoy doing outside under the night sky. Have children make nighttime pictures using black paper and colored chalk. Then have them write or dictate sentences telling about their pictures. Display their work on the Nighttime bulletin board.

Materials
- Colored chalk
- Black construction paper

Signs Around Us

Display Night Lights poster. Tell children that this poster shows some things the boy and Golden Bear might see if they were up late. Briefly discuss the poster with children, focusing attention on the various signs and reading them for children. Encourage children to draw pictures of signs from the poster and signs they have seen. Help them add words to the signs as needed.

Portfolio Opportunity

Save one of the activities on this page as writing samples.

3

Instruct
and
Integrate

Cross-Curricular Activities

Science

Shining Stars

Materials

- picture books about stars and constellations
- black construction paper
- white crayons or chalk

Display pages 28 and 29 and ask what the boy and Golden Bear see. (the first star) Invite children to share their experiences with star gazing. Then display pictures of stars and constellations. Copy one or two constellations, such as The Big Dipper or Orion the Hunter, onto the chalkboard. Mention that some groups of stars, called *constellations*, make pictures in the sky. "Connect the stars" to help children see the pictures these constellations make.

Distribute black construction paper and white crayons or chalk. Invite children to create their own constellations. Suggest that they "connect their stars" to make pictures and to write, or dictate, names for their constellations. Display the constellations in the classroom.

Art

Cloud Art

The boy and Golden Bear saw clouds that looked like fish. Have children go cloud gazing or even close their eyes and imagine big puffy clouds that look like different animals or even objects. Have them make cloud pictures and write or dictate a sentence telling about them.

TIPS: It may be easier for children to draw the outline of the animal or object and then place the cotton inside the outline. Also show them how to lightly pull the cotton apart into strips before gluing onto the paper.

Materials

- white cotton balls
- construction paper
- markers and glue

Music

Night Music

Invite children to sing "Twinkle, Twinkle, Little Star" with you. Then invite children to listen and sing along as you play other nighttime songs. You might, for example, play the following: "Good-Night, Irene," "Taps (Day Is Done)," or a lullaby such as "All the Pretty Little Horses" or "Give My Heart Ease," both found in *Shake It To the One That You Love Best: Play Songs and Lullabies from Black Musical Traditions.*

Invite children to share other nighttime songs they may know. Encourage children to teach the songs to the class.

Students Acquiring English Encourage children to share night music from their own culture.

Materials
- recordings of nighttime songs
- record player or cassette player

Art

Night Light Houses for Golden Bear

Invite children to make their own night lights by following these steps:

1 Cut the bottom off a clean milk carton.

2 Tape construction paper around a clean, empty milk carton.

3 Cut out doors and windows for your night light house.

4 Tape Golden Bear in one of the windows.

5 Shine a flashlight into the house to make a night light for Golden Bear.

Materials
- one quart milk carton for each child
- construction paper
- tape
- scissors
- small teddy bear cutouts

BIG BOOK

SELECTION:

Where Does the Brown Bear Go?

by Nicki Weiss

Other Books by Nicki Weiss

Barney Is Big

An Egg Is an Egg

On a Hot, Hot Day

Surprise Box

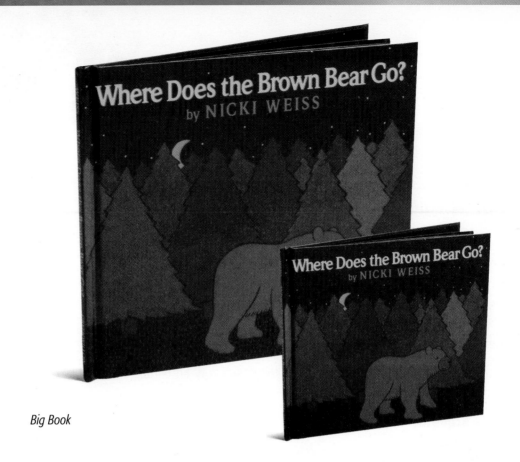

Big Book

Little Big Book

- ● **ALA Notable Children's Book**
- ● **Horn Book Fanfare**
- ● **SLJ Best Books of the Year**
- ● **Library of Congress Children's Books of the Year**
- ● **Best Books for Children**

Selection Summary

As night falls, one by one the animals leave. Where are they going? Where do the cat, the monkey, and the camel go at night? Where do the stray dog, the seagull, and the brown bear go? Why, they are all on their way home. It's only at the end of the story that we realize home is in the arms of a sleeping child, and the animals are really stuffed toys.

Lesson Planning Guide

	Skill/Strategy Instruction	Meeting Individual Needs	Lesson Resources
1 Introduce *the* Literature **Pacing: 1 day**	**Shared Reading and Writing** Warm-up/Build Background, T164 Shared Reading, T164 Shared Writing, T165	Choices for Rereading, T165	**Poster** When All the World's Asleep, T164 *Literacy Activity Book* Personal Response, p. 95
2 Interact *with* Literature **Pacing: 1-2 days**	**Reading Strategies** Self-Question, T166 Evaluate, T166, T176 Summarize, T168, T174, T176 Think About Words, T170, T172 **Minilessons** ✔ Initial *g*, T167 ✔ High-Frequency Word: *go*, T169 ✔ Noting Details, T171 ✔ Recognizes two words that are alike, T173 ✔ High-Frequency Word: *a*, T175 Initial *h*, T177	**Students Acquiring English**, T167, T171, T172, T178, T179 **Extra Support**, T166, T169 **Challenge**, T168, T175 **Rereading and Responding**, T178–T179	**Letter, Word, and Picture Cards,** T167, T169, T175, T177 **Story Props**, T179, H5 *Literacy Activity Book* Language Patterns, p. 96 **Audio Tape** for Nighttime: *Where Does the Brown Bear Go?* See the Houghton Mifflin **Internet** resources for additional activities.
3 Instruct *and* Integrate **Pacing: 1-2 days**	**Reading/Listening Center,** Comprehension, T180 Phonics/Decoding, T181–T182 Concepts About Print, T183 Vocabulary, T184 Listening, T185 **Language/Writing Center,** Oral Language, T188 Writing, T189 **Cross-Curricular Center,** Cross-Curricular Activities, T190–T191	**Extra Support**, T180, T181, T183, T184, T188 **Challenge**, T182, T188, T189 **Students Acquiring English**, T180, T181	**Posters** When All the World's Asleep, T183 Night Lights, T188 **My Big Dictionary,** T181 **Game** Mix-and-Match Letter Sounds, T182, H9 **Letter, Word, and Picture Cards,** T181, T182, T184 *Literacy Activity Book* Comprehension, p. 97 Phonics/Decoding, p. 99 Vocabulary, p. 100 Tear-and-Take, pp. 101–102 **Audio Tape** for Nighttime: *Where Does the Brown Bear Go?*

✔ *Indicates Tested Skills. See page T105 for assessment options.*

Introduce *the* Literature

Shared Reading and Writing

INTERACTIVE LEARNING

Warm-up/Build Background

Sharing Poetry
- Display the poster for "When All the World's Asleep" and read it aloud.

- Talk about where the different animals in the poem go at night. Ask children where they think bugs and butterflies and caterpillars creep when all the world's asleep. Discuss the animal homes named in the poem.

- Read the poem again, encouraging children to join in as they are able.

Shared Reading

LAB, p.95

Preview and Predict
- Display *Where Does the Brown Bear Go?* and read the title. Tell children that Nicki Weiss drew the pictures and wrote the words for the story.

- Briefly discuss the cover illustration, pointing out the bear and the time of day. Ask children to predict where the bear might be going. Promote discussion by rereading the lines about the bear in the poem "When All the World's Asleep."

- Display and read aloud pages 4-7 of the story. Ask children to predict what the story will be about. You might model with a Think Aloud.

Think Aloud

The title asks *Where does the brown bear go?* But the first few pages of the story ask where a cat and a monkey go. I think this story will ask where many different animals go at night.

- Encourage children to predict what animals they will read about.

Read Together
- Invite children to read the story with you, joining in on the rhyming words and any other words they know.

- Pause now and then for children to comment on the illustrations and to check whether their predictions match what happens in the story.

- After reading page 21, pause for children to predict where home is for all the animals. Then read to the end of the story to check their predictions.

Personal Response

Have children complete *Literacy Activity Book* page 95 to show their favorite place mentioned or shown in the story.

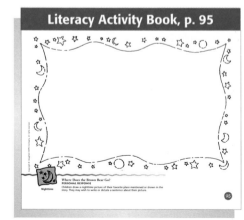

Literacy Activity Book, p. 95

Shared Writing: *A Class Story*

Brainstorming

Have children recall the names of animals they read about in the theme *In the Barnyard*. Suggest that children write a story about where other animals go at night. Have them begin by brainstorming animals' names and where they sleep.

Farm Animals	Where They Sleep
hen	henhouse
pig	pig pen
cow	barn
duck	pond

Drafting

Have children contribute sentences to the class story. Encourage them to use the language pattern from *Where Does the Brown Bear Go?* for ideas. As you record their suggestions, encourage children to supply the initial consonants for words that begin with *b* and *g* as well as these known letters: *m*, *s*, *h*, and *d*.

Then model for children how they might think about an ending for the story.

Think Aloud

How should the story end? It's good to think of several different ideas and then choose the best one. One idea is to have the animals go to a place where real animals go. Or the animals could really be stuffed animals and go to a make-believe place like to bed or to a toy box.

Publishing

Write the verses on separate sheets of drawing paper. Have volunteers illustrate the scenes. Then bind the pages together to make a class book for the Reading and Listening Center.

Choices for Rereading

Rereadings provide varied, repeated experiences with the literature so that children can make its language and content their own. The following rereading choices appear on page T178.

- Word Clues
- Recognizing Language Patterns
- Noting Details
- Listen and Read!

Interact *with* Literature

BIG BOOK

When the lights go down
On the city street,
Where does the white cat go, honey?
Where does the white cat go?

4

When evening settles
On the jungle heat,
Where does the monkey go, honey?
Where does the monkey go?

6

Reading Strategies

▶ **Self-Question**
  Evaluate

Student Application Recall how good listeners and readers think about what happens in a story so they will understand it. They ask questions and make predictions about the things they will learn and they also ask questions after reading to see if they understand and remember the story. Review questions children might ask to help them understand and evaluate this story:

- Does this make sense?

- Is this what I thought would happen?

- Is this a place where a real (animal's name) might live?

Purpose Setting

Invite children to reread the story with you, paying attention to the picture clues and the places where the different animals live. Have them stop and evaluate what they have read at different points in the story.

QuickREFERENCE

Vocabulary

Multiple-Meaning Words Point out that one meaning for the word *honey* is "a sweet syrup made by bees," and that some people use the word as a nickname for people they think are sweet like honey.

 Extra Support

Phrase Meaning Children may need help understanding the phrase *when the lights go down.* (when the lights are off; when it is dark out.)

Visual Literacy

Direct attention to the city street. Note the word written on the storefront and read it aloud. *(bakery)* Ask what other stores the cat might pass on city streets.

Phonics/Decoding

Initial *g*

Teach/Model

Display Magic Picture Card *ghost*.

Have children name the picture, listening for the beginning sound. Mention that Magic Picture *ghost* can help them remember the sound for *g*.

Display page 6 of the story. Ask children to listen as you read aloud the last sentence. Have them listen for a word that begins with the sound for *g*. *(go)*

Practice/Apply

Provide children with Letter Cards for *g*. Ask them to hold up their letters when they hear a word that begins like *ghost* and *go*. Say these words:

gum	game	pine
good	dot	goose
red	gold	goat

SKILL FINDER Naming *G* Words, page T181

Journal

Suggest that children keep track of the animals they read about in the story. Have them write or draw a picture to record each one. Children can use their lists or pictures to help summarize the story.

MEETING INDIVIDUAL NEEDS
Students Acquiring English

Phrase Meaning If children are confused, help them to understand that *evening settles* is another way of saying that night has come.

High-Frequency Word Review

Have a volunteer frame the word *the* on page 6 and name the letters in the word from left to right. Ask children to count how many times the word *the* appears on the page. *(three)*

2

Interact *with* Literature

Reading Strategies

 Summarize

Student Application Discuss how good readers think about the important parts of a story to help them remember it. Ask children to use the illustration on pages 8 and 9 to summarize what has happened in the story so far. If needed, invite children to think about why the cat and the monkey are pictured again on pages 8-9. Check to be sure that they understand that this picture brings together the two animals described so far and answers the questions posed on those pages.

They are on their way.

8

When shadows fall
Across the dune,
Where does the camel go, honey?
Where does the camel go?

10

QuickREFERENCE

**Challenge**

Point out the crescent moon in the illustrations. Use a paper plate and one cut in half to illustrate a full and half moon. Have children make a chart of these three phases of the moon.

Vocabulary/Phonics Review

Ask children to listen for a word that begins with the sound for *d* as you read page 10. Explain that a *dune* is a hill of sand. Ask children where they might see dunes. (at a beach, in the desert)

They are on their way home.

9

11

High-Frequency Word: *go*

TESTED SKILL

Teach/Model

Call on a volunteer to read the last sentence on page 10. Frame the last word in the question. Tell children that this is the word *go*. Display the Word Card *go* and read the word aloud. Ask:

- How many letters are in *go*?

- What letter does *go* begin with? End with?

Practice/Apply

Display this sentence:

Where do you go at night?

Read the sentence with children, asking a volunteer to frame the word *go*. Then invite children to complete the following sentence frame to answer the question:

I go _____.

SKILL FINDER   Reading *A* and *Go* Sentences, page T184

Extra Support

Phrase Meaning Note that *when shadows fall* is yet another way to let the reader know that it is night. Compare this phrase to *when the lights go down* and *when evening settles.*

Science Link

Encourage children to tell what they know about deserts. If necessary, explain that deserts are large areas of land where few plants grow. They are usually very sandy and dry.

Interact
with
Literature

Reading Strategies

▶ **Think About Words**

Discuss how children could figure out the word *moon* on page 12.

The text says:
When the junkyard is lit
By the light of the moon,

- **What makes sense** This word names something that lights up the junkyard at night. When I think of things that give light outdoors at night, I think of a lantern, the moon, and a campfire.

- **Sounds for letters** What letter does this word begin with? *(m)* Does *lantern* begin with the sound for *m*? Does *moon*? Does *campfire*?

- **Picture clues** I see a moon in the picture on page 13. I think the word is *moon*.

Have children reread the sentences on page 12 with you. Ask if the word *moon* makes sense.

When the junkyard is lit
By the light of the moon,
Where does the stray dog go, honey?
Where does the stray dog go?

12

They are on their way.

14

QuickREFERENCE

Vocabulary

Word Meaning Have children use picture clues to tell what a *junkyard* is. Mention that a *stray* dog is a dog that doesn't have an owner. Ask why a stray dog might stay around a junkyard. (to look for scraps of food and a place to sleep)

13

They are on their way home.

15

Comprehension

Noting Details

TESTED ✓ SKILL

Teach/Model

Ask children what they notice about the place each animal goes from in the story. (Each place is different.) Mention to children that they can use clues in the words and the pictures to learn more about the places in which the animals are found.

Think Aloud

When I read a story, I look for clues in the words and pictures to help me understand what I am reading. The words tell me that a stray dog is in the junkyard. The picture shows a dog in front of many broken things. I see a lamp that someone has thrown away and a broken TV set. The words and pictures help me understand what a junkyard is like.

Practice/Apply

Invite children to review other pages in the story. Ask them to use word and picture clues to tell more about the place each animal leaves.

SKILL FINDER

Noting Character and Setting Details, page 180

Minilessons, Themes 1, 3, and 7

MEETING INDIVIDUAL NEEDS
Students Acquiring English

Animal Names Use pages 14 and 15 to help children acquiring English review the names of the animals mentioned in the story so far: *dog, camel, monkey, cat.*

Interact
with
Literature

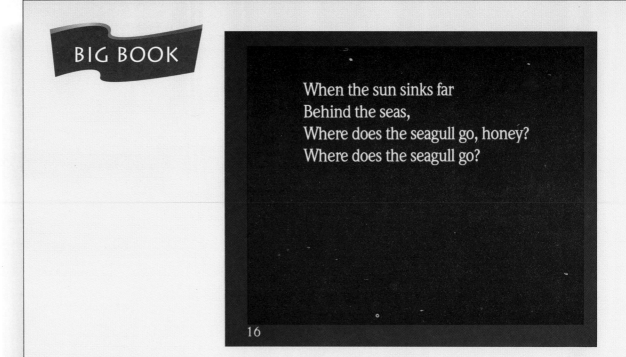

BIG BOOK

When the sun sinks far
Behind the seas,
Where does the seagull go, honey?
Where does the seagull go?

16

When night in the forest
Disguises the trees,
Where does the brown bear go, honey?
Where does the brown bear go?

18

QuickREFERENCE

Students Acquiring English

Invite children acquiring English to share the animals' names from the story in their native languages.

17

19

Concepts About Print

Recognizes Two Words That Are Alike

TESTED SKILL

Teach/Model

Display page 18 of the story. Point to the last two lines on the page. Frame *Where* in the third line and read it aloud. Have a volunteer find the word *Where* in the last line. Ask the volunteer how he or she knew the word was *where*. Paraphrase the response with a Think Aloud.

Think Aloud

I can tell if two words are the same by looking at the letters and comparing them one at a time. (Point to each letter in turn, first with the *where* on the third line and then with the *where* on the last line.) The first letters are both *w.* The next letters are both *h*; the next *e*; the next *r*; and the last *e*. The two words are the same because they have the same letters in the same order.

Practice/Apply

Have partners work together to compare the other matching words in the last two lines on page 18. They should compare the words letter for letter.

SKILL FINDER

Recognizing Words That Are Alike, page T183

Vocabulary

Word Meaning Tell children that *disguises* means "changes the way a thing looks." Ask if they have ever worn a costume, or disguise. Ask how the night disguises the trees. (The trees might look like some other shape, such as a tall bear.)

Science Link

Have children use picture clues to compare the forest on page 19 to the jungle on page 7. How are a forest and a jungle alike? How are they different?

Interact *with* Literature

Reading Strategies

▶ **Summarize**

Student Application Ask children how they can use the picture on pages 20-21 to summarize the story. Before briefly summarizing the story, encourage them to note:

- This page shows all of the animals from the story.

- The animals appear in the same order that they were introduced in the story.

They are on their way.

20

The stars are bright and <u>a</u> warm wind blows
Through the window tonight, honey,
Through the window tonight....

22

QuickREFERENCE

Math Link

Have children compare the animals they see on pages 20 and 21. Ask which animal is the tallest. Which is the smallest?

They are on their way home.

21

 23

High-Frequency Word: *a*

TESTED SKILL

Teach/Model

Reread the first line on page 22. Call on a volunteer to frame the shortest word in this sentence: *a*.

Display Word Card *a*. Note with children that the word *a* is spelled with just one letter, the letter *a*. Recall with them that they have also learned another one letter word: *I*.

Practice/Apply

Use Word and Picture Cards to construct the following sentence in a pocket chart:

I have a .

Have children read the sentence. Then have them change the Picture Card to tell what other animals the child in the story has. Use Picture Cards: *bear, camel, dog, monkey,* and *bird* (for *seagull*). Have children read their new sentences.

SKILL FINDER — Reading *A* and *Go* Sentences, page T184

QuickREFERENCE

Challenge
MEETING INDIVIDUAL NEEDS

Point out that a home or shelter is something all creatures need. Ask children to think of other things that all living things need. (food, water)

Visual Literacy

Have children look at page 23 to tell what happened to the animals in the story. Guide them in realizing that the animals are really stuffed toys.

Interact
with
Literature

And everyone is home.

24

Reading Strategies

▶ **Summarize**
 Evaluate

Student Application Tell children that good readers think about the most important parts of a story to help them remember it. They also tell whether or not they liked a story. Encourage children to take turns retelling the story and telling how they feel about it. Ask:

- Was the ending a surprise?
- Is this a story you would like a friend to read? Why or why not?

Self-Assessment

Remind children that recognizing story patterns can help them understand and remember a story. Have children ask themselves:

- Did I find it helpful to stop and think about what had happened and what might happen next?
- What clues did I use to decide what would happen next in the story?

QuickREFERENCE

Visual Literacy

Help children understand the perspective from which the picture is drawn. Guide them in realizing that they are outside the child's home, looking in the window.

Phonics/Decoding

Initial *h*

Teach/Model

Display Picture Card *horse.* Have children name the picture and tell what beginning sound they hear in this word. (the sound for h)

Ask children to listen as you read the last sentence in the story. Have them listen for a word that begins with the sound for *h.* Read: *And everyone is home.*

Have a child frame the word *home* on page 24. Confirm with children that the word begins with the letter *h.*

Practice/Apply

Ask children to listen for a word that begins with the sound for *h* as you reread the sentences on page 22. Frame the word *honey* and have the initial letter identified.

SKILL FINDER

Minilesson, Theme 5

Interact with Literature

Rereading

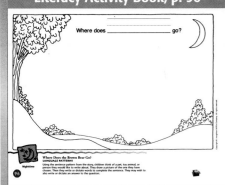

Literacy Activity Book, p. 96

Informal Assessment

Use the Story Talk or the retelling activity to assess children's general understanding of the selection.

Choices for Rereading

Recognizing Language Patterns

LAB, p. 96

As children read the story with you, have them note the language pattern. Help them recognize that the question about each animal has a pattern of first naming a place and then an animal. Direct attention to the repeating lines by pausing for children to read them for you.

Provide practice with the story language pattern by having children complete *Literacy Activity Book* page 96.

Word Clues

As you read the story with children, pause now and then to help them focus attention on selection vocabulary. Ask children to listen for:

- page 4: a word that names a big town (city)
- page 10: a word that names a hill of sand (dune)
- page 12: a word that names a place where people leave their unwanted things (junkyard)
- page 16: a word that names large bodies of water. (seas)

Students Acquiring English Use picture clues to help children with the new vocabulary.

Listen and Read!

Audio Tape for Nighttime: *Where Does the Brown Bear Go?*

Encourage children to read independently by placing copies of the Little Big Book and the Audio Tape in the Reading and Listening Center. Invite children to chime in with the tape as they read the story individually or in small groups.

Noting Details

Help children note details about the story setting by pausing after rereading each spread for them to describe what the setting looks like. Encourage children to use word and picture clues to tell how the animal might feel in the setting as it begins to make its way home and how anxious each animal might be to get there.

Responding

Choices for Responding

Story Talk

Place children in groups of two or three, and have them respond to the following:

- Who do you think the "honey" in the story is? Does anyone in your family have a special nickname for you?

- If a family member was telling the story to you, what animals would they include? Do you sleep with these animals?

Retelling *Where Does the Brown Bear Go?*

Invite children to place the animals on the prop board as they retell *Where Does the Brown Bear Go?* Encourage them to tell where each animal began its journey home and where it ended up.

Students Acquiring English You could use the story props to make sure the children understand the different animals.

Materials
- Story Retelling Props stick-on animals and prop board (See Teacher's Handbook, page H5.)

Add New Animals

Briefly discuss the end of the story with children. Have them think of other stuffed animals the child might have and list their suggestions on the board. Encourage children to tell where these animals' homes might be and draw pictures to show them in their settings. Children can use the story's language pattern to ask where the animals go at night.

Home Connection

Encourage children to draw a picture of the procession of animals in the story. Suggest that they share their drawings with their families to retell the story.

Portfolio Opportunity

Literacy Activity Book page 96 or any of the drawing and writing activities may be saved as writing samples.

Instruct *and* Integrate

SK19

Literacy Activity Book, p. 97

Informal Assessment

- As children complete the activities on T180, note their ability to identify details in the words and pictures.
- As children complete the activities on T181, note the ease with which they are able to recognize and identify words that begin with *g*.

Comprehension

Practice Activities

Noting Character and Setting Details

LAB, p. 97

Extra Support Review the story characters and their settings with children. Have them use word and picture clues to name the animals and tell what each animal's setting is like. Then have children complete *Literacy Activity Book* page 97 to recall story details.

Noting Details About Characters

Recall with children that the animals in the story are really stuffed animals. Have children use picture details to tell how the real animals differ from their stuffed counterparts. Invite children to draw pictures to illustrate these differences.

Students Acquiring English Help children to make a chart of similarities and differences between these two groups.

Settings in Other Stories

Have children recall the story *Ira Sleeps Over*. Encourage children to revisit the story with you to look for details in the words and pictures that tell about the story's setting. Children might comment on:

- Ira's house
- Reggie's room
- Ira and Reggie's street

Invite children to review other books they have read to look for details about the story settings.

Setting Pictures

Invite children to draw different settings. They may draw settings from the story or other settings of their own choosing. Encourage them to include details in their pictures that would help people know where the setting is. Then have children display their drawings. Classmates can use picture details to then try to guess the settings.

Phonics/Decoding

Practice Activities

Literacy Activity Book, p. 99

Naming *G* Words

LAB, p. 99

MEETING INDIVIDUAL NEEDS

Extra Support Display Picture Cards *boy, guitar,* and *girl*. Name the pictures with children. Explain that you are going to say a sentence and leave out a word. Children can supply the word by saying the picture that makes sense and begins with the sound for *g*. Read: *"I have a teddy bear," said the* _____. Help children understand why *girl* is the correct choice.

Repeat the procedure with Picture Cards *goat, guitar, bike* and this sentence: *He can play the* _____. Similarly help them understand why *guitar* is the correct choice in this sentence.

Then have children complete *Literacy Activity Book* page 99 to practice identifying words that begin with the sound for *g*.

Students Acquiring English Go over the name of each item in the picture on the activity page as well as the items on the Picture Cards.

Materials
- Picture Cards: *bear, boy, girl, guitar, goat, bike*

Where Do the Pictures Go?

Clip a letter card to each shoe box. Then provide a small group of children with the Picture Cards for *d, h, m, s, b,* and *g*. Have children take turns choosing a Picture Card, naming it, and placing it in the box with the letter that stands for its beginning sound.

Materials
- Picture Cards for *d, h, m, s, b,* and *g*
- Letter Cards for *d, h, m, s, b,* and *g*
- six boxes

My Big Dictionary

Display page 16 of *My Big Dictionary*. Read the words on the page aloud to children, pointing to the initial *g* and emphasizing the sound /g/ as you read. Then invite children to point to the pictures and identify the words. They might enjoy drawing their own dictionary page showing pictures of things that begin with the sound for *g*. Encourage them to use temporary spellings to label the drawings on their page.

My Big Dictionary

Portfolio Opportunity

For a record of children's understanding of noting details, save their work from Noting Details About Characters. Also keep *Literacy Activity Book* page 99 as a record of their work on initial /g/*g* words.

3

Instruct *and* **Integrate**

Phonics/Decoding

Practice Activities

Spelling *G* and *B* Words

Display Picture Cards for *boat* and *goat* along the chalkboard ledge. Write __*oat* two times on the board. Have children name the pictures and write *g* to complete the word that begins with the /g/ sound and *b* to complete the word that begins with the /b/ sound. Ask children to read the words.

Mix-and-Match Letter Sounds

Materials
● Game: Mix-and-Match Letter Sounds (See Teacher's Handbook, page H9.)

Invite two to four children to play the game to reinforce letter-sound correspondence.

Materials
● Word Cards: *a, A, go, Go, have, Have, I, I, my, My, said, Said, the, The*

Word Memory

Provide small groups of children with Word Cards to play Word Memory:

● Players put the shuffled cards face down on a table in rows and columns.

● Players take turns turning over two random cards, reading the words, and telling whether or not the words match.

● If a match is made, the words are removed from play.

● The player with the most cards at the end of the game wins.

"G" Name Game

MEETING INDIVIDUAL NEEDS

Challenge Have children play this name game in groups. Get them started by saying: "I'm going to the zoo to see a . . ." and then add a word such as *gorilla*. A child then repeats what you said and adds another word — for example, "I'm going to the zoo to see a gorilla and goat." Continue the game having different children add words that begin with *g*. Take turns until the sentence has three or four new words and then switch to another setting, such as a toy store.

Informal Assessment

As children complete the activities, observe whether they can identify two words that are alike.

Concepts About Print

Practice Activities

Recognizing Words that Are Alike

MEETING INDIVIDUAL NEEDS

Extra Support Display pages 20 and 21 of the story. Point to the word *They* on page 20 and read it aloud. Ask children if they can find the word *They* on page 21. Have a volunteer find the word and frame it. Ask how that child knew the word was *They.*

Help children compare the words letter for letter. Then call on partners to compare other words on pages 20-21.

Searching for Words

Display the poster "When All the World's Asleep," inviting children to reread the poem with you. Then provide four groups of children each with a different word from the poem. (These words appear more than once in the poem: *can, do, inside, the*.) Have them find out how many times their word appears in the poem. Suggest that children match the words letter for letter.

Materials
• Poster "When All the World's Asleep"

Word Boundaries: First and Last Letter

Display page 4 and invite a volunteer to read the word *the* in the sentence *Where does the white cat go*? Point to the first letter in the word and have children name it. Then point to the last letter in the word and have children name it. Follow the same procedure for the other words in the sentence. Turn to several other pages and invite volunteers to identify words they know and to name the first and last letters.

Instruct *and* Integrate

Vocabulary

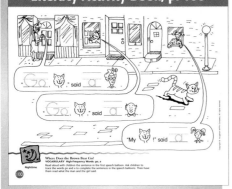

Literacy Activity Book, p. 100

Materials
- Word Cards: *a, go, have, I, my, said, the*
- Picture Cards: *boy, cat, dog, girl,* and others for children to make their own sentences.

Informal Assessment

As children complete the activities, note how easily they are able to recognize and read the high-frequency words. Also observe how effectively they listen to directions.

Practice Activities

Reading *A* and *Go* Sentences

LAB, p. 100

 Extra Support Display Word Cards *a* and *go*, and have children read them aloud. Show children how to create sentences using Word and Picture Cards.

I have a [cat], said the [boy].
Go, [cat], go.

Have children read the sentences. Then invite them to complete *Literacy Activity Book* page 100 to practice reading the high-frequency words.

Play *A* and *Go* Tic-Tac-Toe

Have children work with partners to play Tic-Tac-Toe. Instead of writing X's and O's, however, they should write the words *a* and *go*. As children write each word, they should read it aloud.

Going Home

Prepare a simple board game using the high-frequency words *I, my, said, the, have, go,* and *a*. Provide children with sets of word cards for these words. Have pairs of children race to the finish by drawing a word card, reading the word, and advancing to that space on the board. The first child to reach HOME wins.

GO		the	have	a
I		go		said
my		a		my
said	the	have		HOME

Tear-and-Take Story

LAB, pp. 101-102

Have children remove the *Literacy Activity Book* page, fold it to make a book, and read the story. Then suggest that they take their books home and read them to family members.

My Bear, My Bug

Listening

Listening Activities

They Are Going Home

Use the story pattern to enlist children's help in cleaning up the classroom at the end of the day. Have children listen carefully for their assignments:

When the day is done
In our classroom,
Where do all the blocks go, Jenny?
Where do all the blocks go?

When the day is done
In our classroom,
Where do all the paints go, Adam?
Where do all the paints go?

Ask the Characters

Have children brainstorm a list of questions they might like to ask the animal characters. Record their suggestions on the chalkboard. Have children take turns role-playing the animals to answer the questions you pose as the interviewer.

The Brown Bear
1. What do you like to do during the daytime?
2. Do you get scared at night?
3. What other animals are your friends?

Listen and Read!

Audio Tape for Nighttime:
Where Does the Brown Bear Go?

Use copies of the Little Big Book along with the Audio Tape. Have children follow along, listening for rhyming words and joining in on the lines and words that are the same.

Portfolio Opportunity

Record children's work on the high-frequency words by keeping *A* and *Go* Tic-Tac-Toe.

Instruct *and* Integrate

Independent Reading & Writing

Have a Hug

Have a Hug
by Andrew Clements

This story provides practice and application for the following skills:

■ **High-Frequency Words:** *a, go, have*

■ **Phonics/Decoding Skills:** Initial *b* and *g*; phonogram *-ug*

■ **Cumulative Review:** Previously taught decoding skills and High-Frequency Words

Informal Assessment

As children read aloud *Have a Hug* and complete other activities, note whether they begin to recognize the High-Frequency Words at sight.

Observe children to see if they can:

● Apply left to right directionality when reading

● Select books about a particular topic for reading

● Make an attempt to write about their own experiences

INTERACTIVE LEARNING

Independent Reading
Watch Me Read

Preview and Predict

● Display *Have a Hug*. Point to and read the title and the author's and illustrator's names.

● Briefly discuss the story's cover. Ask children what time of day it is and how they know.

● Take a "picture walk" through page 7 of the story. Help children match the family members in the pictures to the rebuses in the sentences: *father, mother, grandmother, sister*. Mention that the brother is telling the story.

● Ask children to predict what the story will be about. Ask if they think the brother will offer his sister a hug.

Read the Story

● Invite children to read independently to find out if their predictions match what happens in the story.

● After reading the story ask:
How does the story end?
Did anything about the ending surprise you?

Rereading

● Have children reread the story with partners to note details in the pictures. Suggest that one child read the words, while the other tells what's happening in the pictures. Children can then exchange roles to read the story again.

● To help children develop oral language skills, encourage them to add dialogue to the story as they reread it with partners. What else might the boy say to keep from going to bed? What else might his family say?

Responding

● Encourage children to draw and write about a family member they like to hug before going to bed at night.

● Ask children to draw another family member the boy might hug before bed. Suggest they label their pictures: *"Have a hug," I said.*

Student Selected Reading

Sharing Nighttime Favorites

Invite children to bring in their favorite "nighttime" story. Set aside time to speak with each child about his or her favorite book. Ask the child to tell:

- what words they would use to describe the character(s)
- where the story takes place
- if the story is real or make-believe

Children may also enjoy retelling their stories to the class, using the pictures as prompts.

Student Selected Writing

Starry, Starry Night

Have children decorate the classroom ceiling with their thoughts on nighttime.

- Have each child trace and cut out a star shape.
- Ask children to print their names on one side of the star.
- Invite them to write, or dictate, a sentence that tells what they like best about nighttime.
- Attach the stars to string and hang them from the ceiling.

Books for Independent Reading

Encourage children to choose their own books. They might choose one of the following titles.

Have a Hug
by Andrew Clements

Golden Bear
by Ruth Young
illustrated by Rachel Isadora

Where Does the Brown Bear Go?
by Nicki Weiss

Have children read these selections silently or aloud with a partner.

Children can also choose Little Big Books and Watch Me Read books from previous themes.

See the Theme Bibliography on pages T100–T101 for more theme-related books for independent reading.

Ideas for Independent Writing

Encourage children to write on self-selected topics. For those who need help getting started, suggest one of the following activities:

- a **sign** for an "open all night" store
- a **caption** for a nighttime picture
- a **message** to a favorite cuddly toy

Portfolio Opportunity

Save examples of the writing children do independently on self-selected topics.

3

Instruct *and* **Integrate**

Oral Language

Choices for Oral Language

Setting the Scene

Extra Support Recall the settings children read about in *Where Does the Brown Bear Go?* List the settings, and have children brainstorm other animals they might see in these settings.

Place	Animal
City street	cat, dog
Jungle	monkey, tiger, snake
Desert	camel, snake, lizard
Junkyard	dog, cat, mouse
Sea	seagull, whale, dolphin
Forest	bear, squirrel, deer, fox

A Nighttime Story

Challenge Display page 5 of the story. Invite children to comment on how dark and lonely the city streets look at night. Mention to children that in many towns, everything closes at night, and everyone goes home.

Then display the poster Night Lights. Mention that in big cities and towns, some places stay open late, and even all night. Invite children to study the Night Lights scene. Encourage them to create a short oral story to tell about some of the things they see.

In the Daytime

Engage children in a discussion about what the story animals might have been busy doing during the day. Have them think about these questions:

- What does the animal eat?
- What does the animal do?
- Who might the animal meet?

Encourage children in each group to pantomime the animal in action during the day. The other children can guess which animal the group is acting out and try to guess what the animal is doing.

Informal Assessment

Choose from among the activities on this page to informally assess children's oral language skills. Also observe whether their writing reflects an understanding of letter-sound correspondence.

 # Writing

Choices for Writing

Where Do They Go? Stories

Children may want to make their own books, based on the story. Provide each child with the following sentence frames printed on the top half of a sheet of drawing paper:

**When the lights go down
In our big town,
Where does _____ go, honey?
Where does _____ go?**

Have children brainstorm names for animals and people they might write about. Ask them to choose one, and print it in the blank spaces of each sentence. Then have them draw a picture on the bottom half of the page to show where the animal or person goes. Provide children with additional sentence frames to write about more animals and people. When ready to bind the books, provide a concluding page that reads:

**They are on their way.
They are on their way home.**

Writing an Invitation

Challenge Children can plan for the Class Sleep-Over Party by inviting someone to come and read a bedtime story. Have children choose one or two people and help you design the invitation(s).

Cuddly Toy Name Tags

Invite children to make name tags for their own cuddly toys. Have them write their names on one side of the label and the name and description of their cuddly toy on the other side. Children can save the tags to put on their animals that they bring in for the class sleep over.

Portfolio Opportunity

Save children's work on *Where Do They Go?* Stories as a record of their progress in writing about story ideas.

Cross-Curricular Activities

Social Studies

Day and Night Around the World

★★★ **Multicultural Link** Children have been reading about where different animals go at night. Ask if anyone knows where the sun goes at night.

Use a globe and a flashlight to demonstrate that when our part of the world is dark, the sun is shining on another part of the world.

- Using the globe, show children where they live. Then point to a country on the other side of the world, for example China or India.

- Tell children that when it is nighttime where they live, it is daytime for people in these countries.

- Ask them to talk about what children on the other side of the world might be doing while the class is sleeping.

Materials
- globe
- flashlight

Science

Where Real Animals Sleep

Invite children to name different animals and talk about where they sleep at night. Display pictures from nonfiction books on the subject. Encourage children to draw one of the animals in the place it sleeps at night. Have them write, or dictate, a sentence about their pictures.

Compile children's drawings into a class book for the Reading and Listening Center. Encourage children to think of a title for the book and to make a cover for it.

Materials
- nonfiction picture books about real animals

Art

Brown Bear Keepsakes

Provide each child with a large cut out of a teddy bear.

- Invite children to add features to the teddy bear, such as eyes, nose, mouth, and pads on the hands and feet.

- Cut out for children a one to two inch oval in the center of the bear's stomach to act as a frame for the child's photo.

- Turn the bear face down and tape the child's photo over the oval.

If you have available an instant camera, you might wish to photograph each child individually.

Materials
- sturdy brown construction paper
- crayons or markers
- scissors
- tape
- class photo of each child

Health/Nutrition

Edible Clay

Invite children to make peanut butter clay. Have children mix the ingredients in a large bowl until the dough is smooth. Then divide the dough and have children shape it into cats, monkeys, camels, dogs, seagulls, bears, or moons and stars. Invite children to eat their creations.

Teacher Note: The recipe makes about twenty creatures, depending on their size. Left-over dough, and children's creations, can be refrigerated and eaten during the Class Sleep-Over Party. If so, you might wish to postpone the activity until the day preceding the event.

Materials
- 2 cups smooth peanut butter
- 3 cups instant powdered milk
- 6 tablespoons honey
- large mixing bowl

Theme Assessment Wrap-Up

Reflecting/Self-Assessment

Copy the chart below to distribute to children. Ask them which stories in the theme they liked best. Then discuss what was easy for them and what was more difficult as they read the selection and completed the activities. Have children put a check mark under either *Easy* or *Hard*.

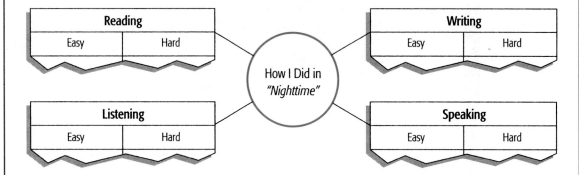

Reading	
Easy	Hard

Writing	
Easy	Hard

How I Did in
"Nighttime"

Listening	
Easy	Hard

Speaking	
Easy	Hard

Monitoring Literacy Development

There will be many opportunities to observe and evaluate children's literacy development. As children participate in literacy activities, note whether each child has a beginning, a developing, or a proficient understanding of reading, writing, and language concepts. The Observation Checklists, which can be used for recording and evaluating this information, appear in the *Teacher's Assessment Handbook*. They are comprised of the following:

Concepts About Print and Book Handling Behaviors
- Concepts about print
- Book handling

Emergent Reading Behaviors
- Responding to literature
- Storybook rereading
- Decoding strategies

Emergent Writing Behaviors
- Writing
- Stages of Temporary Spelling

Oral Language Behaviors
- Listening attentively
- Listening for information
- Listening to directions
- Listening to books
- Speaking/language development
- Participating in conversations and discussions

Retelling Behaviors
- Retelling a story
- Retelling informational text

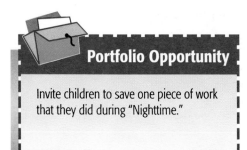

Portfolio Opportunity

Invite children to save one piece of work that they did during "Nighttime."

Choices for Assessment

Informal Assessment

Review the Observation Checklists and observation notes to determine:

- Did children's responses during and after reading indicate comprehension of the selections?

- How well did children understand the skills presented in this theme? Which skills should be reviewed and practiced in the next theme?

- Did children enjoy the cooperative activities related to the major theme concept?

Formal Assessment

Select formal tests that meet your classroom needs:

- *Kindergarten Literacy Survey*
- *Integrated Theme Test*
- Theme Skills Test for "Nighttime"

See the *Teacher's Assessment Handbook* for guidelines for administering tests and using answer keys and children's sample papers.

Portfolio Assessment

Evaluating Progress in Emergent Reading

Emergent readers demonstrate their abilities in many ways. At this level, observation, conferencing, and drawings provide valuable evidence of emerging reading abilities. Here are several ways children can demonstrate their understanding:

- Observe children during independent reading time to note children who have developed book handling skills and reading behaviors.

- Observe children's decoding behaviors as they play with rhyming words, recognize environmental print, and use temporary spelling.

- Have children draw pictures of what they have heard or read. It's often helpful to ask them to draw the most important part or their favorite part of the story. Children's drawings can also be used as prompts for oral retellings.

- Observe children's personal responses to reading selections. Their work on such things as posters or dramatizations, and their conversation while working, can be good indicators of how well they understood what they read. As you observe, take notes for future reference.

- Use the Emergent Reading Checklist as a guide or record form for your observations.

Managing Assessment

Planning Instruction

Question: How might I use checklist information to plan instruction?

Answer: Try these ideas:

- Use the checklists and your curriculum guides to review the important learning that you want to focus on during instruction. Then examine the checklists and other assessment information to determine which strategies, skills, or learnings you have not covered or that children still need help with. This will help you set instructional priorities.

- Use the information recorded on the checklists to form flexible groups for instruction. For example, you may pull together children who need additional work in a particular area, or you might set up mixed-ability peer groups to support children as they work on projects applying particular skills.

- Review the checklists and your records to identify children for whom you have limited information. Focus on these children over the next couple of weeks. Record your observations.

For more information on this and other topics, see the *Teacher's Assessment Handbook*.

Celebrating the Theme

Choices for Celebrating

Materials

- **Read Aloud Book:** *Ira Sleeps Over*
- **Big Books:** *Golden Bear, Where Does the Brown Bear Go?*

See the **Houghton Mifflin Internet resources** for additional theme-related activities.

Self-Assessment

Have children meet in small groups to discuss some of the things they learned in the theme. Use the following prompts to foster their discussion:

- Which selection in the theme did you like best? Why?
- Name some things you learned about nighttime.

Book Talk

Display the theme books. Ask children to tell about the stories and their characters. Encourage them to choose a class favorite to reread during the Class Sleep-Over Party. Prompt additional discussion by asking:

- How does each book fit the theme: Nighttime?
- What cuddly toy did each book have? Why do you think so many night-time stories include cuddly toys?
- What other books might you choose to go into a Nighttime theme? Why?

Theme Talk

Invite children to share what they've learned during the theme.

- Encourage children to talk about the songs and poems they have sung and read and also the books from the Reading and Listening Center they have enjoyed.
- Discuss how children feel about night-time and whether their feelings have changed.
- Invite children to share their favorite writing projects and activities.

A Class Sleep-Over Party

Help children get organized for the Class Sleep-Over Party. Make sure:

- The room is decorated.
- Invitations have been sent.
- Cuddly toys have name tags.
- Snacks are ready to be served.

Once the guest reader arrives, suggest that children share some of their night-time projects with the storyteller. Invite the storyteller to read a bedtime story to children as they snuggle with their favorite toy. After serving the snacks, have a bedtime sing-along of the theme song, "Twinkle, Twinkle, Little Star."

Teacher's Handbook

TABLE OF CONTENTS

Story Retelling Props

INTERACTIVE LEARNING

Resources
- stand-up characters
- prop stands
- mirror

The Rain Puddle

Children will enjoy using the stand-up animal props and the mirror to retell the story *The Rain Puddle*. Assemble the stand-up animal figures by sliding the bottom edges into the prop stands. Have children take turns standing each animal on the edge of the mirror and telling what the animal sees, says, and does in the story. Encourage children to make sounds to show how the animals in the story are feeling. Children may want to make barnyard scenery to use as a backdrop for the puddle and the animal props.

Materials
- oaktag
- crayons or markers
- craft sticks
- scissors
- glue

The Rain Puddle

For *The Rain Puddle,* make stick puppets by cutting out a silhouette of each story animal from oaktag and gluing it to a craft stick. Children may want to help you color or decorate the paper silhouettes. Supply a mirror for the "puddle." Children can use the puppets to retell the story.

INTERACTIVE LEARNING *(continued)*

Spots Feathers and Curly Tails

Children can retell *Spots Feathers and Curly Tails* by using animal puzzles of a cow, chicken, pig, duck, and horse. To make each puzzle, cut a 10" x 12" rectangle from oaktag. Draw the animals listed above. Make sure to add the characteristic that makes each animal unique, such as black spots for the cow. Then cut a simple puzzle shape with a single vertical line through the picture. Mix the pieces and make them available to children. Have children retell the story using the pieces to recall which animals have spots, feathers, or curly tails.

Materials
- oaktag
- crayons or markers
- scissors
- glue

I Love Animals

Cut out the shape of a head for each of the animals featured in the story *I Love Animals,* or cut out pictures of these animals. Along the top edge of a large piece of oaktag, tape each animal head so that it lies hidden below the edge of the paper but can be folded into view using the tape as a hinge. From left to right, the animals should appear in this order: dog, duck, hen, goat, donkey, cow, pig, pony, sheep, lamb, cat, and turkey. The large oaktag sheet can then be propped up on a low desk in front of a group, and the story can be retold by showing one animal at a time.

Materials
- oaktag
- crayons or markers
- scissors
- glue

Story Retelling Props

Materials
- teddy bears

Ira Sleeps Over

For *Ira Sleeps Over,* you may want to bring in two teddy bears or invite students to bring their teddy bears from home. Children can use the stuffed bears as they dramatize the story.

Materials
- teddy bears

Golden Bear

To retell *Golden Bear,* children may enjoy using a very large teddy bear to role-play scenes from the story. Or you may want to encourage children to take turns using their own bears to dramatize different scenes from the story.

INTERACTIVE LEARNING *(continued)*

Where Does the Brown Bear Go?

Children can arrange the stick-on animals on the prop board as they retell *Where Does the Brown Bear Go?* Lean the prop board against an easel or the chalkboard, and then make the stick-on animals available to a group of children. Have them take turns placing the animals on the prop board as they retell the story.

Resources
- stick-on retelling pieces
- prop board

Where Does the Brown Bear Go?

You can create felt board pieces to retell *Where Does the Brown Bear Go?* On construction paper, draw a large bed, a white cat, a monkey, a camel, a dog, a seagull, and a brown bear. Cut out the pictures and paste a piece of felt material onto the back of each one. Children can arrange the figures on a felt board as they retell the story.

 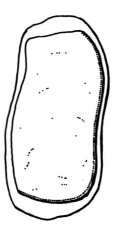

Materials
- construction paper
- felt
- felt board
- crayons or markers
- scissors
- glue

Games

Resources
- Around the Barnyard game board
- Tokens

Around the Barnyard

Players: Two

Preparation Name each picture on the game board with children: *barn, door, hay, cow, house, dog, bird, horse, corn, basket, cat, duck.* Name each picture on the spinner with children: *car, desk, hose, bell.* Have each child choose a group of tokens of one color.

Directions In turn, each player:

1. Spins the spinner.

2. Names the picture shown on the spinner.

3. Finds on the board a picture whose name begins with same sound.

4. Places a token on the picture if one is found. If all pictures that begin with the sound have been covered, the player does not put down a token.

5. Continues playing until all pictures on the board are covered. The player who has more tokens on the board wins.

Variation Children can work together as a group to cover the board.

INTERACTIVE LEARNING *(continued)*

Additional Game Idea: Fun on the Farm

Players: Two–Three

Here is an additional game idea to reinforce listening for beginning sounds.

Preparation Draw on each index card one of the following pictures: *barn, bird, bug, basket, cat, cow, corn, cucumber, duck, dog, hen, horse, hay, hoe.* Name the pictures with children. Then divide the cards among the players.

Directions In turn, each player:

1. Places on the table any pairs of cards with pictures whose names have the same beginning sound.

2. Names one of his or her remaining unpaired pictures.

3. Asks another player to listen for the sound at the beginning of the picture name and to look at his or her cards for a picture whose name begins with the same sound. If the other player has a matching card, he or she gives it to the player who named the picture.

4. Places the pair of pictures with the matching beginning sound on the table.

5. Continues playing until one player has paired all of his or her pictures. The player with the most pairs wins.

Materials
- Index cards

Games

Resources

- Animals at Night game board
- Tokens

Animals at Night

Players: Two–Four

Preparation Have each child choose a group of tokens of one color. Teacher points to each animal in turn and says its name: *beaver, bear, duck, dog, hen, horse, monkey, mouse, seal, sea gull.*

Directions In turn, each player:

1. Spins the spinner.

2. Names the letter shown.

3. Finds and identifies an animal whose name begins with the letter sound and places a token on that animal. If all the animals for a letter on the spinner have already been covered, the player does not put down a token.

4. Play continues until all the animals are covered. The player with the most tokens on the board wins.

INTERACTIVE LEARNING *(continued)*

Additional Game Idea: Mix-and-Match Letter Sounds

Players: Two–Four

This is another game idea to reinforce listening for beginning sounds.

Preparation Name the letters and pictures with children. Put the Letter Cards face down in a group and mix them up. Do the same with the Picture Cards.

Directions In turn, each player:

1. Picks one letter card and one object card.

2. Names the letter on the letter card and then says the name of the object. If the sound of the letter and the beginning sound of the object match, the player keeps the matched pair. Unmatched cards are turned face down again in the appropriate groups.

3. Play continues until all the letter cards and object cards are matched. The player with the most matched pairs wins.

Materials
- Letter Cards: 2 of each *b, d, h, m, g,* and *s*
- Picture Cards: 2 for each letter above, for example, *bat, bird*

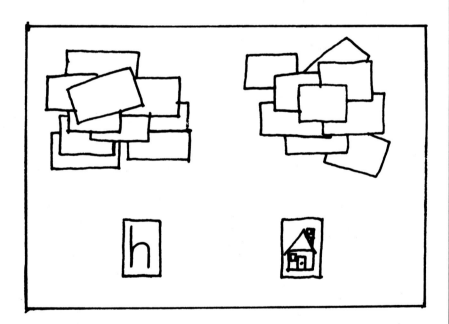

Old MacDonald

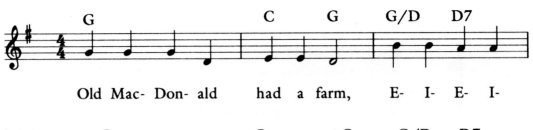

Old Mac- Don- ald   had a farm,   E- I- E- I-

O! And   on his farm he   had some chicks,   E- I- E- I-

O! With a   peep, peep here, and a   peep, peep there,

Here a peep, there a peep,   e- very- where a peep peep.   Old Mac- Don- ald

had   a   farm,   E- I- E- I-   O!

Eensy Weensy Spider

The een-sy ween-sy spi-der went up the wa-ter

spout, Down came the rain __ and

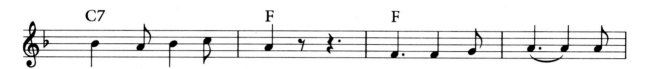

washed the spi-der out, Out came the sun __ and

dried up all the rain, and the een-sy ween-sy

spi-der went up the spout a- gain.

Five Little Ducks

Five lit- tle ducks that I once knew,

Fat ones, skin- ny ones they were too, But the one lit- tle duck with the

feath- ers on his back, He ruled the oth- ers with his

quack, quack, quack, quack, quack, quack! quack, quack, quack!

He ruled the oth- ers with his quack, quack, quack.

Twinkle, Twinkle, Little Star

Audio-Visual Resources

Adventure Productions
3404 Terry Lake Road
Ft. Collins, CO 80524

AIMS Media
9710 DeSoto Avenue
Chatsworth, CA
91311-4409
800-367-2467

Alfred Higgins Productions
6350 Laurel Canyon
Blvd.
N. Hollywood, CA
91606
800-766-5353

American School Publishers/SRA
P.O. Box 543
Blacklick, OH
43004-0543
800-843-8855

Audio Bookshelf
R.R. #1, Box 706
Belfast, ME 04915
800-234-1713

Audio Editions
Box 6930
Auburn, CA 95604-6930
800-231-4261

Audio Partners, Inc.
Box 6930
Auburn, CA 95604-6930
800-231-4261

Bantam Doubleday Dell
1540 Broadway
New York, NY 10036
212-782-9652

Barr Films
12801 Schabarum Ave.
Irwindale, CA 97106
800-234-7878

Bullfrog Films
Box 149
Oley, PA 19547
800-543-3764

Churchill Films
12210 Nebraska Ave.
Los Angeles, CA 90025
800-334-7830

Clearvue/EAV
6465 Avondale Ave.
Chicago, IL 60631
800-253-2788

Coronet/MTI
108 Wilmot Road
Deerfield, IL 60015
800-777-8100

Creative Video Concepts
5758 SW Calusa Loop
Tualatin, OR 97062

Dial Books for Young Readers
375 Hudson St.
New York, NY 10014
800-526-0275

Direct Cinema Ltd.
P.O. Box 10003
Santa Monica, CA 90410
800-525-0000

Disney Educational Production
105 Terry Drive,
Suite 120
Newtown, PA 18940
800-295-5010

Encounter Video
2550 NW Usshur
Portland, OR 97210
800-677-7607

Filmic Archives
The Cinema Center
Botsford, CT 06404
800-366-1920

Films for Humanities and Science
P.O. Box 2053
Princeton, NJ 08543
609-275-1400

Finley-Holiday
12607 E. Philadelphia St.
Whittier, CA 90601

Fulcrum Publishing
350 Indiana St.
Golden, CO 80401

G.K. Hall
Box 500, 100 Front St.
Riverside, NJ 08057

HarperAudio
10 East 53rd Street
New York, NY 10022
212-207-6901

Hi-Tops Video
2730 Wiltshire Blvd.
Suite 500
Santa Monica, CA 90403
213-216-7900

Houghton Mifflin/Clarion
Wayside Road
Burlington, MA 01803
800-225-3362

Idaho Public TV/Echo Films
1455 North Orchard
Boise, ID 83706
800-424-7963

Kidvidz
618 Centre St.
Newton, MA 02158
617-965-3345

L.D.M.I.
P.O. Box 1445,
St. Laurent
Quebec, Canada H4L
4Z1

Let's Create
50 Cherry Hill Rd.
Parsippany, NJ 07054

Listening Library
One Park Avenue
Old Greenwich, CT
06870
800-243-4504

Live Oak Media
P.O. Box 652
Pine Plains, NY 12567
518-398-1010

Mazon Productions
3821 Medford Circle
Northbrook, IL 60062
708-272-2824

Media Basics
Lighthouse Square
705 Boston Post Road
Guildford, CT 06437
800-542-2505

MGM/UA Home Video
1000 W. Washington
Blvd.
Culver City, CA 90232
310-280-6000

Milestone Film and Video
275 W. 96th St.,
Suite 28C
New York, NY 10025

Miramar
200 Second Ave.
Seattle, WA 98119
800-245-6472

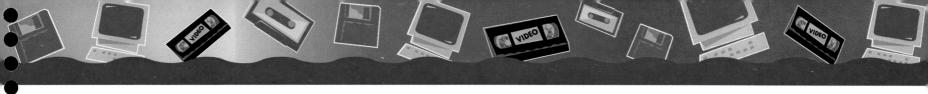

Audio-Visual Resources *(continued)*

National Geographic
Educational Services
Washington, DC 20036
800-548-9797

The Nature Company
P.O. Box 188
Florence, KY 41022
800-227-1114

Philomel
1 Grosset Drive
Kirkwood, NY 13795
800-847-5575

Premiere Home Video
755 N. Highland
Hollywood, CA 90038
213-934-8903

Puffin Books
375 Hudson St.
New York, NY 10014

Rabbit Ears
131 Rowayton Avenue
Rowayton, CT 06853
800-800-3277

Rainbow Educational Media
170 Keyland Court
Bohemia, NY 11716
800-331-4047

Random House Media
400 Hahn Road
Westminster, MD 21157
800-733-3000

Reading Adventure
7030 Huntley Road,
Unit B
Columbus, OH 43229

Recorded Books
270 Skipjack Road
Prince Frederick,
MD 20678
800-638-1304

SelectVideo
7200 E. Dry Creek Rd.
Englewood, CO 80112
800-742-1455

Silo/Alcazar
Box 429, Dept. 318
Waterbury, VT 05676

Spoken Arts
10100 SBF Drive
Pinellas Park, FL 34666
800-126-8090

SRA
P.O. Box 543
Blacklick, OH
43004-0543
800-843-8855

Strand/VCI
3350 Ocean Park Blvd.
Santa Monica, CA 90405
800-922-3827

Taliesin Productions
558 Grove St.
Newton, MA 02162
617-332-7397

Time-Life Education
P.O. Box 85026
Richmond, VA
23285-5026
800-449-2010

Video Project
5332 College Ave.
Oakland, CA 94618
800-475-2638

Warner Home Video
4000 Warner Blvd.
Burbank, CA 91522
818-243-5020

Weston Woods
Weston, CT 06883
800-243-5020

Wilderness Video
P.O. Box 2175
Redondo Beach, CA
90278
310-539-8573

BOOKS AVAILABLE IN SPANISH
Spanish editions of English titles referred to in the Bibliography are available from the following publishers or distributors.

Bilingual Educational Services, Inc.
2514 South Grand Ave.
Los Angeles, CA
90007-9979
800-448-6032

Charlesbridge
85 Main Street
Watertown, MA 02172
617-926-5720

Children's Book Press
6400 Hollis St., Suite 4
Emeryville, CA 94608
510-655-3395

Childrens Press
5440 N. Cumberland Ave.
Chicago, IL 60656-1469
800-621-1115

Econo-Clad Books
P.O. Box 1777
Topeka, KS 66601
800-628-2410

Farrar, Straus, & Giroux
9 Union Square
New York, NY 10003
212-741-6973

Harcourt Brace
6277 Sea Harbor Drive
Orlando, FL 32887
800-225-5425

HarperCollins
10 E. 53rd Street
New York, NY 10022
717-941-1500

Holiday House
425 Madison Ave.
New York, NY 10017
212-688-0085

Kane/Miller
Box 310529
Brooklyn, NY
11231-0529
718-624-5120

Alfred A. Knopf
201 E. 50th St.
New York, NY 10022
800-638-6460

Lectorum
111 Eighth Ave.
New York, NY 10011
800-345-5946

Santillana
901 W. Walnut St.
Compton, CA 90220
800-245-8584

Simon and Schuster
866 Third Avenue
New York, NY 10022
800-223-2336

Viking
357 Hudson Street
New York, NY 10014
212-366-2000

Index

Boldface page references indicate formal strategy and skill instruction.

high-frequency words. *See* High-frequency words.

last letter in written words, **T73**, **T85**, **T183**

recognizing words that are alike, **T173**, **T183**

turning pages, T88

word boundaries, **T155**, **T183**

word collage, T57, T85

word find, T85

Conclusions, drawing, T25, T28. *See also* Inferences, making; Themes 2, 7, 12.

Constructing meaning from text. *See* Interactive Learning.

Cooperative learning activities, T27, T36, T37, T52, T53, T56, T80, T81, T82, T86, T93, T125, T127, T130, T151, T152, T156, T178, T179, T181, T182, T188

Cooperative reading. *See* Reading modes.

Creative dramatics

acting out scenes, songs, and stories, T17, T27, T80, T124, T150

demonstrating, T20, T25, T72, T76, T78, T90

dramatizing, T124, T150

finger play, T16, T36

hand/body motions, T90

pantomime, T17, T55, T122, T128, T150, T188

playing teacher, T57

puppetry, T80

role-playing, T21, T27, T28, T33, T88, T124, T125, T148, T157, T185

sound effects, T27, T42, T52, T88

Creative response. *See* Responding to literature.

Creative thinking, T25, T28, T30, T52, T62, T74, T125, T128, T130, T134, T185, T188, T189

Creative writing. *See* Writing, creative.

Critical thinking, T12, T17, T18, T20, T24, T27, T28, T33, T36, T37, T38, T46, T50, T53, T54, T59, T61, T62, T63, T74, T75, T78, T81, T82, T87, T88, T111, T113, T118, T119, T151, T164, T171, T173, T179

Cross-cultural connections. *See* Multicultural activities.

Cross-curricular activities

art, T16, T22, T57, T62, T131, T160, T161, T191

health, T77, T146, T191

math, T32, T41, T43, T62, T92, T130, T141, T174

movement, T33, T63

multicultural activities, T18, T39, T49, T119, T147, T190

music, T63, T93, T114, T139, T161

science, T19, T23, T25, T32, T41, T43, T47, T62, T63, T77, T93, T115, T130, T140, T141, T143, T144, T160, T169, T173, T190

social studies, T33, T39, T45, T50, T92, T118, T131, T190

visual literacy, T25, T38, T40, T42, T44, T46, T48, T51, T117, T118, T119, T166, T175, T176

See also Centers.

Cue systems. See Decoding, word attack; Think About Words.

Cultural diversity. *See* Multicultural activities.

D

Decoding skills

phonics

beginning sounds

b, T29, T56, **T139**, T140, T150, T153, T154, T165, T181, T182

c, T41, T56

d, T29, **T69**, **T83**, T87, T96, T137, T154, T168, T181

f, T19, T29, T41, T119

g, **T167**, **T181**, T182

h, T29, **T45**, **T55**, **T56**, T70, **T71**, T87, T96, T116, T119, T137, **T177**, T181

j, T29

k, T19, T29

l, T74

m, T44, T56, T78, T87, T141, T154, T155, T165, T170, T181

p, T19, T29, T74, T119

r, T119

s, T19, T22, T29, T56, T87, T144, T181

t, T29, T119, T127

phonograms

-at, **T77**, **T84**

-ug, **T141**, **T154**, T186

Think About Words, T44, T70, T140, T144, T170

word attack,

cloze, T22, T44, T51, T55, T58, T70, T116, T169, T181

picture clues, T18, T22, T39, T66, T70, T78, T116, T121, T140, T141, T142, T143, T144, T170, T171, T178, T180

Details, noting, T17, T42, T63, **T171**, T178, **T180**, T186. *See also* Main idea and supporting details; Themes 1, 3, 7.

Dialogue, adding, T30, T186

Diaries and journals. *See* Journal.

Dictionary. *See* My Big Dictionary.

Drafting. *See* Writing skills.

Drama and dramatic play. *See* Creative dramatics.

Drawing. *See* Illustrating.

Drawing conclusions. *See* Conclusions, drawing.

E

Evaluating literature. *See* Literature, evaluating.

Evaluation. *See* Assessment options, choosing.

Extra Support. *See* Individual needs, meeting.

F

Fantasy/realism, distinguishing, T18, T20, T136, **T143**, T152. *See also* Themes 4, 10.

Fluency

reading, T52, T58

oral reading, T84

speaking, T30, T158, T188

writing, T31

Functional literacy. *See* Literacy, functional.

T50, T51, T52, T54, T55, T57, T58,
T69, T70, T71, T75, T80, T82, T83,
T84, T85, T90, T111, T112, T114,
T115, T118, T122, T124, T126,
T127, T128, T136, T138, T141,
T150, T152, T158, T166, T180,
T181, T182, T183, T184, T188,
T189. *See also* Individual needs,
meeting.
Limited English proficient students.
See Students acquiring English.
Linking literature
 to health, T77, T146
 to math, T41, T43, T141, T174
 to multicultural studies, T18, T39,
  T49, T119, T147
 to music, T33, T114, T139
 to literature, T142, T146
 to science, T19, T23, T25, T41,
  T43, T47, T77, T115, T140,
  T141, T143, T144, T169, T173
 to social studies, T39, T45, T50,
  T118
 to visual literacy, T25, T38, T40,
  T42, T44, T46, T48, T51, T117,
  T118, T119, T166, T175, T176
Listening ability, T114, T138
Listening activities
 content
  for alliteratives, T19, T29, T69,
   T70, T74
  to an audiotape, T12, T52,
   T80, T87, T91, T150, T178,
   T185
  to bedtime rhymes, T157
  to bedtime stories, T106
  for beginning sounds, T87,
   T116, T119, T127, T137,
   T139, T140, T144, T150,
   T153, T167, T170, T177,
   T181, T182
  to descriptions by classmates,
   T60
  to discussion, T54, T63, T79,
   T82, T106, T130, T141,
   T154
  to favorite-animal speech, T90
  to guest readers, T106, T194
  to jokes, T90
  to literature discussion, T26,
   T27, T38, T42, T46, T50,
   T53, T68, T74, T78, T88,
   T111, T114, T125, T136,

T138, T142, T146, T148,
T158, T164, T176
  to music, T33, T93, T138,
   T158, T161
  to nursery rhymes, T59
  to oral reading, T59. *See also*
   Rereading.
  to a poem, T36, T66, T110,
   T134, T155, T164
  to questions, T59
  to retelling, T124, T125, T150
  to rhyming words, T127, T137,
   T141, T150
  to riddles, T61, T84
  to shared writing, T31, T37
  to singing, T12, T16, T36, T63,
   T106, T127
  to story talks, T27, T53, T81,
   T124, T125, T150, T151,
   T179
  to storytelling, T17, T26
  to teacher modeling, T18, T19,
   T20, T21, T24, T25, T28,
   T39, T41, T51, T60, T69,
   T71, T75, T77, T79, T112,
   T113, T119, T120, T137,
   T139, T143, T145, T169,
   T171, T173, T177
  to teacher read aloud, T16,
   T31, T54, T66, T88, T110,
   T124
  to Think Aloud, T18, T19,
   T20, T24, T37, T39, T41,
   T112, T113, T118, T119,
   T141, T143, T145, T164,
   T165, T171, T173
 purpose
  to analyze and evaluate, T18,
   T20, T26, T27, T42, T46,
   T50, T53, T54, T59, T68,
   T74, T78, T81, T88, T90,
   T111, T114, T120, T124,
   T125, T136, T138, T142,
   T143, T146, T148, T150,
   T151, T157, T171, T176,
   T179
  to build background, T16,
   T36, T66, T110, T134,
   T164
  to categorize/classify, T31,
   T46, T63, T79, T82, T130,
   T158
  to comprehend, T16, T18,

T20, T25, T54, T66, T79,
T93, T110, T112, T124
  to compare characteristics,
   T60, T79
  to compare selections, T53
  to compare sounds, T137to
   develop concepts, T21,
   T38, T41, T51, T79, T113,
   T137, T145, T155, T169,
   T173
  to draw conclusions, T60
  for enjoyment, T90, T93, T157,
   T161, T185
  to gain information, T19, T37,
   T50, T59, T89
  to generate questions, T18
  to identify alliteratives, T19,
   T29, T69, T70, T74
  to identify beginning sounds,
   T87, T116, T119, T127,
   T137, T139, T140, T144,
   T150, T153, T167, T170,
   T177, T181, T182
  to identify phonograms, T77,
   T84, T141, T154
  to identify rhyming words,
   T127, T137, T141, T150
  to introduce selections, T12,
   T16, T106
  to move and mirror, T33, T63,
   T93
  to recognize letters and words,
   T41
  to recognize rhymes, T127,
   T141
  to recognize sounds, T93
  to reread, T21, T26, T38, T52,
   T80, T87, T88, T124, T125,
   T150, T178, T185
  for sharing, T31, T50, T53
  to think critically, T18, T19,
   T20, T24, T37, T39, T41,
   T112, T113, T118, T119,
   T141, T143, T145, T164,
   T165, T171, T173
  to visualize, T28
  to write, T91
Literary appreciation, T16, T27, T53,
 T81, T125, T151. *See also*
 Literature, analyzing.
Literature
 analyzing, T26, T27. *See also*
  Literary devices; Story ele-

during reading, T18, T20, T21,
T25, T46, T48, T69, T71, T72,
T74, T76, T78, T114, T138,
T140

exact words, T41, T90

expression/idioms, T18, T23,
T112, T115, T118, T122, T149,
T166

high-frequency words, **T51**, **T58**,
T68, **T70**, **T75**, T86, T96, **T136**,
T137, T156, T167, **T169**, **T175**,
T184, T186

informal speech, T113, T116

multiple-meaning words, T46,
T48, T51, T138, T166

onomatopoeiac words, T120

phrase meaning, T166, T167, T169

rebus completion, T86

rhyming words, T84, T127, T134,
T137, T150

sound words, T18, T20

synonyms, T116

using word webs, T37

vocabulary chart, T30

word families. *See* Greek word
roots.

word meanings, T18, T20, T21,
T25, T51, T69, T71, T72, T76,
T78, T114, T138, T140, T144,
T170, T173

Vocabulary, selection. *See* High-frequency words. *See also* Language,
concepts and skills; Context,
using; Decoding skills.

W

Watch Me Read books
Have a Hug by Andrew Clements,
T186
The Horse's Hat by Andrew
Clements, T88

Word analysis. *See* Structural analy-
sis; Think About Words;
Vocabulary, extending;
Vocabulary, selection.

Word webs, T37

Words, automatic recognition of. *See*
High-frequency words.

Writer's log. *See* Journal.

Writing
activities
barnyard book, T31

captions, T53, T89, T91, T187
chore chart, T61
class book, T67, T190
class poem, T135
class story, T37, T165
continue the story, T88, T129
description of farm animals,
T31, T61
family-member description,
T186
finishing sentences, T52, T80
group recipe, T91
grow a story, T84
"I Love You" notes, T89
invitations, T89, T91, T189
journal. *See* Journal.
labels, T128, T129, T141,
T151, T186
message to favorite animal,
T187
name tags, T189
pictionaries, T89
picture postcards, T129
rebus completion, T86
rhyming verses, T158
riddle book, T61
science records, T32, T93
scrapbooks, T89
sentences, T26, T125, T126,
T129, T159, T160, T187
signs, T159, T187
star wishes, T159
"What's in the Bag?"
responses, T125
"Where Do They Go?" stories,
T189
word collections, T89
word paintings, T61
copying, T67, T91, T157, T159
creative, T37, T67, T88, T135,
T165, T189
dictated, T27, T30, T31, T53, T57,
T60, T67, T85, T125, T129,
T159, T160, T187
independent. *See* Independent
writing.
modes of organization
classificatory, T31, T61
descriptive, T27, T31, T37, T60,
T61, T67, T89, T91, T93,
T125, T126, T129
expressive, T67, T125, T158,
T159, T187

functional, T89, T91, T159,
T187, T189
informative, T129, T151, T187,
T190
narrative, T37, T84, T86, T129,
T165, T189
shared, T31, **T37**, **T67**, T84, **T135**,
T158, **T165**
Writing skills
brainstorming, T37, T52, T61, T67,
T135, T165, T189
copying, T67, T91, T97, T158
describing, T31, T91
drafting, T37, T67, T135, T165
keeping to topic, T37
prewriting, T37, T67, T135, T165
publishing and sharing, T31, T37,
T61, T67, T135, T165
See also Language and usage.